The New
Dynamics of
Goal Setting

Also by Denis Waitley

Books

The Psychology of Winning
The Winner's Edge
Seeds of Greatness
Being the Best
The Joy of Working
The Double Win
Timing Is Everything
Empires of the Mind
The New Dynamics of Winning

Audiotapes

The Psychology of Winning
Seeds of Greatness
The Double Win
The Inner Winner
Being the Best
How to Build Your Child's Self-Esteem
The Course in Winning
The New Dynamics of Winning
The Psychology of Human Motivation

The New Dynamics of Goal Setting

Flextactics for a

Fast-Changing World

Denis Waitley

William Morrow and Company, Inc.
New York

It is the policy of William Morrow and Company, Inc., and its imprints and affiliates, recognizing the importance of preserving what has been written, to print the books we publish on acid-free paper, and we exert our best efforts to that end.

Library of Congress Cataloging-in-Publication Data

Waitley, Denis.
    The new dynamics of goal setting : flextactics for a fast-changing
world / Denis Waitley.
        p.   cm.
    ISBN 0-688-12668-5
    1. Success in business.   2. Career development.   3. Goal
(Psychology)   4. Adaptability (Psychology)   I. Title.
HF5386.W157   1996   95-52121
650.14—dc20   CIP

Printed in the United States of America

FIRST EDITION

1   2   3   4   5   6   7   8   9   10

CONTENTS

CONTENTS

It Could Happen to You (If It Hasn't Already)

It was a typical bitter-cold winter's day in Boston when Jeff Sampson got the news from a colleague that his company might soon lay off one thousand employees. Jeff, a thirty-five-year-old aeronautics engineer, had worked for the aeronautics corporation for twelve years, and as a middle manager he had his eye on becoming a department head. He and his wife had been counting on moving into a larger home that would accommodate their family of five. While awaiting final word on who would get the ax, Jeff grew nervous. Work in his department had been slow for the last two months and middle managers were always the first to go. . . .

Across the continent in Seattle, the day was less cold but cloudier. Brian Harris, who for ten years had managed a number of major accounts for a Los Angeles–based ad agency, was concerned that the weakening of direct mail as an advertising vehicle was going to cause some personnel changes at his company. Although his work had been outstanding and the clients loved him, he was not at the main office in L.A. and that could make him vulnerable. There might be some hard choices coming up. Would he have to pull his two kids out of school and move away from a city he'd grown to love? Or . . .

In Southern California at that very moment, Linda Royer was also considering her future. She was doing well enough with her own interior-design business when a friend told her of an opportunity that sounded off the wall but that somehow intrigued her. It would involve spending several months in Russia as an assistant to a Russian entrepreneur who was importing American medical supplies. The amounts of money involved in the Russian importing business dwarfed what she was used to, and this was a chance to get in on something big at the beginning. Should she give up the small business she'd created for a high-risk proposition? Or should she content herself with limited opportunities and ignore the opportunity to participate in a major international enterprise?

No matter where you live or what kind of work you do, you've probably heard of people facing precarious situations like those described above. It may have happened to close friends or members of your family, or it may have happened to you. All around America, people are having to readjust their views on what to expect for themselves and for their families. With corporate downsizing, working for one company for many years of your life is just not realistic these days. With the changing nature of American business, companies have been forced to restructure themselves to become more efficient and compete at a global level. With the growth of technology, the world is advancing at a rapid rate. According to Michael Treacy, co-author of *The Discipline of Market Leaders,* a typical $1 billion company may be staffed by seven thousand people today, but within a few years that same company is going to have a total of one thousand employees.[1] That means six thousand people are going to be looking for work!

According to the Bureau of Labor Statistics, only 15 percent of workers recently laid off can expect to return to the same job. More than 6 million workers will continue in part-time jobs because they won't be able to find full-time work. Another million or so have simply given up looking for work. This means that 17 million people, or almost 12 percent of the labor force, are unemployed and, very likely, extremely unsatisfied with their lives.

A survey by the management consulting firm Kepner-Tregoe finds that downsizing has become the rule rather than the exception at many big companies. More than a third of the corporations that had downsized during the past five years expect to continue to streamline their organizations during the coming year. Defense cutbacks will add to the losses for years to come; the total of jobs eliminated in that sector alone could be as high as 2.6 million by 1997.

The changes we are facing are not limited to the workplace. With the increase in divorce, remarriage, alternative living arrangements, and other lifestyle situations, families need to be able to remain open and flexible to any circumstance. Recently, I had the opportunity to study and work with a number of the most successful Japanese companies including Toyota, Sony, and Fujitsu. At a meeting of top executives in one organization, the CEO told me the Japanese have an old saying that is relevant to the way we live our lives today: "If you haven't seen a man or woman for three days, look them over very carefully when you next encounter them, for they will have changed dramatically during that three-day period."

One secret behind Japan's competitive success is that nation's mastery of "flexible manufacturing technology"—the ability to adapt manufacturing processes to changing customer and market requirements, and to do it fast. The idea that each of us can make incremental, continuous improvements every day— that we can literally *reinvent* ourselves—is the heart of Japan's economic philosophy of Kaizen, which means getting better, doing more, little by little every day.

Masaaki Imai, an international management consultant and the author of a provocative book on Kaizen, says that change is something most of us take for granted but do little to anticipate or manage. In contrast, the most successful Japanese companies have very directly recognized the importance of change. At a recent executive committee meeting of a large, multinational corporation, for example, the chairman of the board began the meeting: "Ladies and gentlemen, our job is to manage change. If we fail, we must change management." He smiled and everyone in the room got the message.

The New Dynamics of Goal Setting was created for high-performance individuals who know their primary mission in life and are looking for efficient, effective ways of fulfilling that mission. The cutting-edge strategies you'll learn here, which I call *flextactics,* will not only put you on track toward achieving your goals, but will help you remain flexible and focused no matter what obstacles, unforeseen circumstances, or setbacks might appear in your path. Each chapter in this book presents a new flextactic, and the twenty-one-day plan that concludes the book provides a practical model for putting flextactics to work in your life, starting immediately.

In a world of change, flextactics are principles that will remain valid no matter what alterations or disruptions take place in the economy. This is only possible because flextactics are not just things you should do—*rather, they're ways you should think.* In the language of mathematics, they are constants. Just as a physicist can use the speed of light in any equation, you can apply flextactics in any set of circumstances.

Simply put, flextactics are the essence of what we must know in order to be successful, but they are not dusty maxims carved in stone. They are in sync with the newest discoveries in the theories of chaos and complexity, which, in my opinion, provide the best models for explaining the current business environment.

In *The New Dynamics of Goal Setting,* the most exciting discoveries in contemporary science are combined with the insights into human behavior and productivity that have come from my own twenty-five years of experience in studying peak performers. The result is an innovative self-study course designed to provide you with the action steps you need to stay focused and flexible in your goal setting and goal-achievement process, no matter what stage you're at in your personal success plan.

Ronald McGimpsey, when he was a top executive at BP America, once said, ''The dynamics of the industrial marketplace are such that people can no longer be assured that coming to work and just doing what they're told eight A.M. to five P.M. will carry them to retirement age. They're in competition with the person who sits at the next desk or who sits in a similar desk in some other country. They've got to be flexible and adaptable.''

Are flextactics effective? Let's look at what they did for the three people we met earlier. Jeff Sampson was indeed laid off by the aerospace company—but because he had foreseen this obstacle in his path, he was able to transform what could have been a setback into an opportunity. Jeff wasn't the only engineer who had been laid off, and with two of his former colleagues at the aeronautics firm he began seeking financing for a new kind of small, self-navigating cargo plane. It would have the ability to fly in poor weather conditions, from snowstorms to sandstorms, using radar similar to that of the Patriot missile launched by Americans during the Gulf War. Once Jeff and his partners raised sufficient capital, they planned to start their own company, which they hoped would eventually employ thousands of workers.

Jeff Sampson's presentations of the cargo plane idea were successful, and he got his money. He was lucky—or rather, he created luck for himself. Instead of drowning in the seas of unemployed and unprepared workers who were let go only a few months after the first rumors of downsizing, he was able to quickly rebound thanks to a unique method of goal setting. He utilized the powerful techniques you'll learn in this book to chart a course that will carry him successfully through the rest of his career.

Brian Harris didn't wait for the ax to fall, nor did he have to leave Seattle. Instead, he quit the L.A. agency and started his own operation. What's more, because of the excellent work he'd done over the years, some major clients eagerly followed him. Within two years Brian's agency was one of the largest in the Northwest—and Brian himself had won a trade association award for one of his highly successful direct mail campaigns.

Linda Royer also risked giving up what she had in order to get something better. It was a sensible risk, and she won big. Within a few weeks of arriving in Russia, Linda was talking on the phone with leaders in government and international business. She was seeing new places, doing new things, and meeting new people. She even fell in love!

Quick thinking and flexibility allowed Jeff, Brian, and Linda to strike out on their own, and when you apply the flex-tactics you'll find in this book, there's no reason you can't be equally successful. You'll also learn how to start a journal and how to make it a key component of your success. You'll discover how visualization, a leading-edge tool of contemporary behavioral science, can become a powerful force for achievement in your personal and professional life. And there's much more as well.

The New Dynamics of Goal Setting shows exactly how to make your success happen. Let's get started!

The New
Dynamics of
Goal Setting

CHAPTER ONE

Flextactic: Make Flexibility the Key to Your Success

Chaos: Friend or Foe?

Perhaps it's inherent in human nature to seek the security of living and working in a known environment, but in order to achieve success today you simply can't remain in your carefully constructed comfort zone. Instead, you must learn to become comfortable with the unfamiliar and the unknown. It's what I call *changing your personal paradigm,* and it may be the most challenging aspect of reaching your life goals.

Derived from the Greek word *paradeigma,* meaning model, a paradigm is a way of understanding the world. It's a pattern or set of guidelines that influences the way you look at your life.

Today we are facing an incredible "paradigm shift" in the way we approach our most important life goals. The great French anthropologist and philosopher Claude Lévi-Strauss once said that the difference between so-called primitive societies and modern society was like the difference between a clock and a railroad locomotive. The clock is designed to make the same cyclical motion again and again at exactly the same speed; the locomotive, however, is designed to get from one place to another—it's supposed to be fast, powerful, and able to haul tremendous loads. Yet even the most impressive railroad engine

1

ever built could not serve as a metaphor for the incredibly fast-paced and constantly changing lifestyle many of us now experience. It seems as if everything—computers, financial transactions, telecommunications—is constantly going faster, and all of us are expected to keep pace.

That's why the concept of flexible goal setting that you'll learn in these pages is so valuable. By putting it to work, you can successfully meet the ever-increasing demands of your personal and professional life. You'll also be able to define and achieve objectives that are uniquely your own, whether that means white-water rafting in Idaho, climbing a mountain in Africa, or just spending more time with your family. In short, the purpose of this book is to guide you toward new outlooks and new courses of action that will make success more frequent and more enduring in every area of your life.

No matter what you set out to accomplish, one thing is certain: You're going to find yourself thinking that the task would be so much easier if only there were more time, or more money . . . or if some obstacle wasn't always getting in the way.

Despite the fact that they're everywhere, obstacles somehow manage to seem totally unnatural. As a result, people try to storm their obstacles as if they were forts that need to be taken. It's better to step back and ask yourself: Did I cause this obstacle by my own actions or lack of them? Did someone else cause this obstacle? Is this obstacle one that grew out of the natural progression of circumstances? These questions may seem a bit academic when you're rushing to meet a deadline or put together a presentation, but in fact they hold the secret to effectively setting and reaching your goals.

The ancient Greeks labeled the universe *Cosmos,* meaning order. Whenever some obstacle appeared to upset the precise balance of nature, they believed it was the work of *Chaos,* meaning the forces of confusion and disarray. What the Greeks didn't know is that chaos is actually a normal and natural element in the design of the universe and is therefore unavoidable in our daily lives as well.

The modern study of chaos began slowly in the 1960s with the realization that simple mathematical equations could model systems as violent as waterfalls and storm patterns. Within these systems, tiny differences in input could quickly become overwhelmingly large differences in output—a phenomenon called "sensitive dependence on initial conditions." In his book *Chaos: Making a New Science,* author James Gleick refers to a phenomenon known as the "Butterfly Effect"—the idea that a butterfly stirring the air today in Beijing, China, can transform the weather next month in New York City.[2] In a complex system with many variables, even an apparently minor factor can become magnified into a controlling element. This fact has extremely important implications for what we can expect in our own lives. It means that we can accurately predict the results of our endeavors only if we know *all* the factors, even the smallest, that are present at the outset, because any one of them might turn into a major influence. Since it's impossible to understand every single initial variable, we must temper our expectations of the future with a realization that absolute certainty and total security are impossible. We simply must learn to live with the question marks.

In traditional science and even in our everyday lives, we have long known that a chain of events can reach a crisis point in which minor elements become greatly magnified. What the science of chaos has taught us is that these points of crisis appear everywhere almost all the time. And where chaos begins, classical science ends.

Since the study of physics began in the ancient world, mankind has been aware of the fundamental unpredictability of natural phenomena such as storms, harvests, and even the often abrupt ending of a human life. In the 1970s and 1980s, mathematicians, physicists, biologists, and chemists began to notice connections between different kinds of irregular occurrences.

Physiologists, for example, found a surprising order in the chaos that develops in the human body during a heart attack, the prime cause of sudden death.

As we move into the twenty-first century, we must be aware that chaos theory has become a shorthand name for a movement that is reshaping the entire scientific establishment. Now that we are aware of chaos, we see it everywhere: a steep drop in the stock market, a column of cigarette smoke breaking into wild swirls, an airliner experiencing turbulence in a clear sky. No matter where we look, the behavior obeys the same newly discovered laws.

What does all this theory mean to you and me in our everyday lives? Simply everything! At present, for example, heart pacemakers are programmed to supply a steady beat. But the human heart actually functions very irregularly—even "chaotically"—depending upon the level of exertion and energy an individual is experiencing at any given moment. So a more effective pacemaker, designed to integrate this erratic phenomenon, might be programmed to make rapid adjustments to the heartbeat when needed.

In goal setting, the old way was to set goals and preprogram specific subgoals and priorities on a list, then check them off one by one as they were accomplished in an organized, step-by-step approach. The twenty-first-century achiever, however, understands that there is a "sensitive dependence on initial conditions." Aware that chaos is always exerting an influence, he or she sets life-forming goals with subgoals that can be adjusted to meet spur-of-the-moment changes and rapidly shifting conditions. Multipurpose flexibility is built into all goals, plans, and activities.

This approach, which is the foundation of flextactics, determines how to fit every new circumstance or experience into your life-forming goals. It's an important aspect of the tactics we'll be discussing throughout this book. Through flextactic planning, any vision of your future can be changed or adapted as the need arises. This method helps alleviate some of the stress caused by not achieving what you thought you should have achieved and, instead, concentrates your energy on creating and fulfilling innovative new goals.

They may not even realize it, but most people have general life goals—such as happiness, security, wealth, acceptance by others, health, and some measure of success—but these goals often remain vague and undefined. A person may be quite busy, and may even be overwhelmed with projects and responsibilities spread out in all directions, but his or her goals are never achieved because they were never properly set in the first place.

Without clear, specific goals, even the most diligent work inevitably turns into nothing more than an unavoidable interruption between weekends.

Thermodynamics and Goal Setting

While it's important to have well-defined goals, it's equally important to keep your goals manageable, and again this can be illustrated by a scientific principle.

According to the First Law of Thermodynamics, the amount of energy in any closed system always remains constant. In other words, the energy put into a system must always be balanced by energy going out. Applied to goal achievement, this First Law of Thermodynamics means that small goals require only small amounts of energy expended to attain the desired result, while creating something of great value or importance demands much more effort. This is a very important principle to keep in mind as you define and attempt to reach your own objectives. Always break them down into subgoals that are easier to reach and easier to adjust because they are incremental. And remember that the results you achieve will be in direct proportion to the effort you apply.

However, consistency is extremely important in your efforts to achieve your goals, because according to the *Second* Law of Thermodynamics, the level of entropy, or disorganization, in any closed system inexorably increases. This means that your capacity for focused energy is always limited, and you need to harness it and maximize it in order to achieve your greatest potential. All of us have an ''energy bank account'' deposited in our bodies as our life force. But we can't make any more deposits into our energy account; we can only make withdrawals. So we should strive to spend our energy as creatively and wisely as we can over the longest possible time span.

Margaret Wheatley, in her book *Leadership and the New Science,* writes that man fears change because ''it uses up valuable energy and leaves us only with entropy.'' Because we unconsciously convince ourselves that the future holds confusion and decline, we seek a sense of security by maintaining the status quo. Even an unsatisfactory present seems better than the frightening prospect of things to come. Wheatley, however, encourages cooperation with a changing world rather than a futile attempt to suppress change. For you, this sense of cooperation can begin with learning to be flexible about your goals. This can start you down the road of constant renewal and away from the stagnation and entropy that result from following a narrowly defined career path.

Managing Your Energy

Goals can concentrate energy: By defining what needs to be done and by setting reasonable time limits in which to do it, goals can bring out the best in you. In this sense, goals are like the rules of games like tennis or baseball. If you try to practice tennis with a net that's too low or with a baseline too far away, you'll never know when you've hit the ball too low or too hard. You may never know the disappointment of missing a shot, but neither will you ever know the satisfaction that comes from playing the game well. In terms of bringing about true accomplishments, the "obstacles" that seem to be standing in the way are really the foundation of our achievements.

Laser technology may be the best example of focused energy that has ever existed. A laser—the word is an acronym for Light Amplification by Stimulated Emission of Radiation—produces a beam of very pure light in which all the waves are exactly the same wavelength.

An individual with focused, concentrated goals is very much like a laser beam. While any ordinary lightbulb can illuminate a general area, laser power can execute a wide variety of spectacular tasks, from performing delicate eye surgery to triggering a thermonuclear explosion. It can carry more than a hundred thousand times more information than a telephone line and can produce twenty thousand lines of print in sixty seconds. It can drill through substances that are as hard as diamond or as soft as rubber.

Scientists believe that in the future, lasers will help propel rockets and starships faster than we can imagine, and more economically than today's airplanes transport us around the country. Yet, thirty years ago no one had ever seen a laser beam.

Laser technology and effective goal achievement are based upon the same scientific principles. When light waves are concentrated and in step they produce a beam of pure light with incredible power. When goals are kept in focus and are approached in orderly progression, they ignite the human mind's awesome creativity and powers of accomplishment.

I've always been fascinated by the fact that while we all say we don't have enough time to achieve our goals, each of us has all the time there is. No one really has a time-management problem. We really have a *focus* problem. We spend too much energy worrying about the things we want to do but can't, instead of concentrating on doing the things we can do but don't.

Your dreams are your creative vision of your life in the future. Dreams are what you would like your life to become. Goals, on the other hand, are the specific events that you intend to make happen. Goals should be just beyond your present reach, but never out of sight.

It's tragic that so many people become mere spectators of life, resigned to experience success vicariously through others' accomplishments. They can see success for others, but they can't imagine it for themselves. Think of your dreams and goals as previews of the coming attractions in your life. This doesn't mean a grade B movie that someone else wrote and directed for you. It means an Oscar-winning epic for which you are the producer, the scriptwriter, and the star performer!

Let's get down to the specifics of goal achievement. Over the past twenty-five years I've discovered four fundamental rules that define peak-performing, personally fulfilled individuals.

Rule One: Believe in Your Dreams and Goals

Successful people believe in the validity of their own dreams and goals, even if dreams are all they have to go on.

The great dancer Mikhail Baryshnikov once said, "I don't try to dance better than anyone else. I only try to dance better than myself." In its most basic form, success is an internal matter. As individuals, we are not born with equal physical and mental attributes, so many of us must come from behind to overcome obstacles that were present in our early family environments. But we all have an equal right to feel the excitement and motivation in believing that we deserve the very best in life. We can all attain the best, but we must make an internal commitment to believe it and achieve it.

Belief, then, is the first key quality, but it cuts both ways like a two-edged sword. Positive belief, in the form of a goal, is the key to unlock the door of success for every human being. Conversely, negative beliefs are the mind-forged locks that can permanently prevent us from ever gaining access to success.

As positive energy, belief is the promise that hoped-for goals will at last be realized. As negative energy, it's the premonition of our deepest fears and unseen feelings of inadequacy. As children, we had fantasies about what we wanted to be when we grew up. As we grew older, we began to narrow the possibilities. Some careers and aspirations seemed beyond our reach. We were advised—or ill-advised as the case might be—by teachers, parents, peers, and other adults, that we couldn't be, shouldn't be, or wouldn't be an expert, leader, or success in this field or that. Over time, many of our targets seemed inaccessible or out of range to us, in our imaginations.

Rule Two: Clearly Define Your Goals

Successful people have clearly defined goals and action plans. They have a specific sense of direction, and that direction is based upon their own desires—not those assigned by someone else.

During the years when he was one of the most powerful men in Hollywood, the late Sam Goldwyn was often asked how he decided which scripts would be turned into movies. "It's simple," he replied. "I make a picture that I want to see. If I like it, there's a chance somebody else will too." Successful people know what they want in their personal and professional lives, and they can describe their plans and objectives in vivid detail. They project their dreams and goals into definitive periods of time, and set their own target dates for achievement.

Close your eyes for a moment and envision where you will be five years from today. Place that image on a movie screen, noticing as many details as you can. Picture what your environment looks like, the people you are with, the clothes you are wearing, the time of year, the color of your hair. Don't censor yourself from imagining whatever comes to your mind. You are now on your way to becoming a successful achiever.

Rule Three: Do What It Takes to Win

Successful people make their plans work. They exert effort, energy, and whatever time it takes to reach their goals.

One night in the winter of 1940, during England's bleakest period of World War II, Winston Churchill was working late with his secretary, Mary Thompson, on an important speech he would be giving the next day. Finally, at 3:00 A.M., the last words were dictated. "There!" declared the prime minister, quite cheerfully. He added, "Don't bother typing this right now, Mary. I won't be needing it until eight in the morning." Years later, Mary Thompson remembered her reaction: "Since there were at least thirty pages of text, Churchill's remark had its amusing side. But the force of his personality and his determination was such that I immediately began work, knowing full well that retyping would take the rest of the night. It was finished before eight, which was all that mattered. He had what he wanted, and I had the personal satisfaction of knowing that I had done my share."

Most people think in terms of an eight-hour day and a forty-hour week. Peak performers don't put any limits on their commitment to success. Their greatest accomplishments are often achieved while the also-rans are resting. Above all, successful people persevere.

While it's important to follow your dreams, it's equally important to exert all your energy to transform your dreams into reality. While many people can articulate their vision, when it comes time to carry out the actions necessary for achievement, they fall short. I'll teach you how to stay on target, even when you think you've come to the end of the road. A key aspect of using flextactics is learning to build resilience—that's why it's important to remember the final rule.

Rule Four: Remain Adaptable to Change

Successful people are adaptable and flexible. They welcome change and the opportunities that always come with it.

With his jutting jaw and gravel voice, Everett Dirksen of

Illinois was the perfect image of a United States senator. "I am a man of fixed and unbending principles," he once intoned, "the first of which is to be flexible at all times."

In a fast-paced, global village, change can't be an occasional episode in the life of an individual, a family, or a professional organization. Change is constant and ongoing. Individuals and organizations with rigid structures will be swept away in obsolescence. Individuals and organizational cultures that can adapt rapidly to change will survive and thrive.

This is the age of self-reliance and self-exploration. Be alert for new opportunities as you progress along your chosen path. Open yourself to the new paradigm of achievement. There's really no other choice. The obviously unacceptable alternative can be summed up by an old Chinese definition of insanity: "Doing what you have always done, in exactly the same way, and expecting a different outcome."

The Story of Eric, Consummate Goal Setter

During a goal-setting seminar I conducted in 1980, I asked the participants to write down and discuss five questions which all centered around their goals. I asked them specifically what they would be doing five years and twenty years in the future, how good their health might be, and what their assets would be. As you can imagine, they all looked stunned when asked to get that specific about their future. All but one person, who was too young to have given up on his dreams!

He was a red-haired, freckle-faced ten-year-old named Eric, whose father had brought him to the program to get some positive input. Instead of input, he gave us all output that put our adult fears and insecurities to shame. While all the grown-ups struggled for answers they had never really focused on before, young Eric volunteered to come up to the podium to share his answers to the series of goal-setting questions.

He said his greatest talents were building model airplanes, doing well in video games, and operating a personal computer. He said he needed improvement in cleaning his room and being nice to his sister. His personal goal for 1980 was to build a model of the space shuttle and his professional goal was to earn four hundred dollars doing yard work for neighbors. For 1981, he said his personal goal was to take a trip to Hawaii and his professional goal was to earn seven hundred dollars for the super-saver airfare and room package offered by the airlines. He said the hardest part of that goal was to get his mom and dad to save enough money for their tickets, so that they could take him.

When asked about his five-year goals, he said: "I'll be fifteen in 1985, in the tenth grade, and I'll be taking a lot of math, science, and computer classes."

Eric had to think for a moment when I asked him about his twenty-year life goals. He said, "In the year 2000, I'll be thirty-three years old then, right? I'll be living in Cape Canaveral, Florida. I'll be a space-shuttle astronaut working for NASA or a communications company putting satellites into orbit. And I'll be in great physical shape. You have to be in good shape to be an astronaut," he finished proudly.

Where is Eric today, the ten-year-old who dared to dream so specifically and vividly about the future back in 1980? He graduated from the Air Force Academy in the class of 1992, entered flight training, and has his sights firmly set on performing well enough as a pilot and officer to become a candidate for the astronaut program before June 2 of the year 2000, which will be his thirty-third birthday!

To envision the future as clearly as Eric did—and to make it happen—requires both imagination and a clear view of reality.

It also takes courage, because there's risk involved whenever we set out to accomplish something in spite of all the obstacles that are sure to block our way. But that risk is well worth taking. In fact, learning to thrive on risk is an essential element in goal achievement, as we'll see in the next chapter.

CHAPTER TWO

Flextactic: Learn to Thrive on Risk

"They're Not Called Terminals for Nothing"

The curious headline above appeared over a small item in *The Wall Street Journal* not long ago. It seems that a Boston-based money-management firm had installed computer terminals with software that could pick stocks. Soon thereafter, the firm fired fourteen people, including two research analysts, four portfolio managers, a stock trader, and a quantitative analyst. "Those employees were doing a good job," the firm's president said. "There were just too many of them."

The kind of shock felt by those abruptly out-of-work people in Boston will, in one form or another, be felt by all of us—because the world we have always known isn't the world we will find ahead. We have entered a new era. It has been called by many names: information society, postindustrial society, the Age of Technology. By whatever name, it's a dramatic departure from the past.

In the 1970s, Alvin Toffler previewed the effects of change in his book *Future Shock*. Toffler accurately predicted that "millions of ordinary, normal people face an abrupt collision with the future ... many of them finding it increasingly painful to keep up with the incessant demand for change that characterizes our time." And in an insightful book with a truly chilling title— it's called *The End of Work*—author Jeremy Rifkin provides a thorough examination of the forces that are transforming the American economy. Yet as Rifkin describes it, what's happening now is simply an extension of the dislocations that have gone on since the beginning of the Industrial Revolution in the eighteenth century, but for the first time the process is affecting white-collar managers as well as workers in the rank and file. For centuries, machines have created unemployment for people who worked with their strong backs or skilled hands, but suddenly machines are also displacing men and women who think for a living. Rifkin quotes Michael Hammer, formerly a professor at MIT and an expert on corporate restructuring, who predicts that up to 80 percent of all middle-management jobs are vulnerable to elimination. And according to *The Wall Street Journal,* downsizing could eliminate between 1 million and 2.5 million jobs a year, with no end in sight.[3]

For many Americans, and for people throughout the world, the future has arrived too soon. A tidal wave of change has swept over their lives, all but obliterating their dreams, sometimes tragically. During the past ten years, for example, nearly 6 million men and women in this country have lost their jobs due to "structural changes" in the economy.

Let me emphasize that these rapid and disruptive changes are not confined to any particular occupational group. They're happening in the service sector of the economy as well as the industrial sector, in newly emerging industries as well as those that have traditionally been mainstays of the economy. They affect not only steelworkers and autoworkers, but defense contractors, real estate developers, middle managers, and top executives of blue-chip corporations.

During the most recent recession, at least half a million white-collar jobs were lost. And despite economic expansion, lower interest rates, low inflation, and government programs to stimulate the economy, major corporations are still in a staff-reduction mode which experts predict will continue indefinitely.

This is because we are experiencing a global revolution, not just a structural change in our own country.

In a *Newsweek* poll, 49 percent of those surveyed said that the United States no longer dominates world business, and 58 percent of those polled reported that it was safer to work for smaller companies than larger ones. Referring to the plight of many large corporations, Ed Lawler, head of the Center for Effective Organizations at the University of Southern California, says, "The reason people are getting a feeling of collapse is because that's exactly what's happening."

"There is no longer any job security in the large companies," comments David Birch, an economist at MIT. "In fact, the situation in the larger companies is now much more erratic than job change in smaller, entrepreneurial operations." Birch's extensive research reveals that the smaller, rapidly growing, highly flexible businesses are creating the majority of new jobs.

Major changes such as these are by no means confined to our professional lives. Studies by the Census Bureau show that adults today undergo at least twice as many important "life changes" as their parents and grandparents did. Once upon a time, a typical American passed through five major life-cycle transitions: childhood, marriage, childbirth, child rearing, and the eventual dissolution of the marriage, usually through the death of a spouse. But today the typical person will have at least twice that many life transitions. Those include a foreshortened time of childhood innocence, a period of independent living before marriage, marriage, divorce, remarriage, and so forth. With divorce ending one out of two marriages, the loss of childhood innocence may be the biggest change of all.

In the previous chapter we saw how the Second Law of Thermodynamics describes entropy as a necessary part of life and presents disorder as the natural condition of all things. When the world is in such a state of flux and is constantly evolving, you have two choices: You can either remain stagnant and be left behind or you can choose to grow with the changing nature of the universe. As Ikujiro Nonaka wrote in an article for *California Management Review,* "In order to renew itself, an organization must maintain itself in a non-equilibrium state at all times." Choosing to grow means choosing to continuously renew and redefine yourself. "Creative disorder" can be the pathway to rejuvenation.

Risk: The Key Ingredient for Achievement

Whether you're comfortable with it or not, risk is going to be part of your personal and professional life from now on. But "risk" isn't the villain that it's often portrayed to be. As you pursue your goals, you can make sensible risk a key ingredient of your achievements.

In the years after the Great Depression, America embarked upon an attempt to eradicate risk. We asked the government to guarantee our savings. We bought billions of dollars' worth of insurance. We sought lifetime employment with cost-of-living increases each year to protect us from inflation. Executives awarded themselves generous "golden parachutes," lest they come out on the losing end of a merger or takeover.

This national experiment had many obvious benefits, but there was also a downside. As risk avoidance became a fixation, we forgot that risk can also be a positive force, that progress can happen when people take chances. Instead of finding total security, we discovered apathy, mediocrity, and reduced opportunity.

Today the national mind-set is shifting once again. We're beginning to see how risk can create rewards. Those who would have entered "safe" careers a generation ago now enter fields that require and encourage risk taking. Suddenly, risk takers are the new heroes.

What does it mean to be a risk taker? If we accept the evidence of magazine profiles and television interviews, it's easy to think that risk takers are larger than life and innately different from everyone else. But if we believe this, we give ourselves an excuse not to act. As a result, people who have absolutely brilliant ideas for new businesses find themselves repeating, ''I'm going to do this, and I'm going to do that.'' But they don't make it happen.

Even those who venture to dip a toe in the pond of risk rarely allow themselves to get used to the water, as psychiatrist David Viscott observes in his book *Risking*.[4] Dr. Viscott points out that since most people have very little experience with risk taking, they often go about it all wrong. In particular, they tend to lose their nerve just when they should be taking decisive action. If even the smallest thing appears to be going wrong, inexperienced risk takers convince themselves that the sky is falling and retreat. When they ought to be going full speed ahead, they're just worrying about how to survive.

Most of us have never become comfortable with risk. Yet to prosper in this new era of change, you've got to take prudent chances. You simply must develop a healthy acceptance of risk.

Determining Your Risk-Taking Style

Healthy risk taking is neither recklessly rolling the dice nor waiting to bet on a sure thing.

Reckless dice rollers usually feel that no matter how hard they try, nothing seems to work out for them. They have never stopped to learn from previous mistakes. They fail to achieve their goals because they haven't confronted the levels of information, experience, or ability necessary for achieving them. They make snap decisions about investments without first investigating them . . . or launch into projects without considering the costs in terms of time, money, and effort. Such people have permanent potential: Because they're always looking for a score on a long shot, they never master the step-by-step building process that leads to lasting achievement. All their plans are really nothing more than invisible lottery tickets. But sensible risk taking isn't based on long odds. Rather, it involves taking a hard look at what you really want, investing lots of long hours and effort, and reaping rewards that are long-lasting.

Security seekers are at the opposite end of the spectrum from the riverboat gamblers. Typically, their lives become increasingly narrow as they grow older. Their education stops when they graduate from school. They have a small, closed circle of friends. They don't move out of their comfort zone unless it's absolutely necessary, and when faced with choices they always choose the path of least resistance. For these no-risk-total-security people, success is simply a matter of avoiding failure. But in reality, *nothing* can guarantee total security. The only absolutely secure person is lying six feet underground. That person's worries are over, but life aboveground is inherently risky.

There is only one big risk you should avoid at all costs, and that's the risk of doing nothing. Doing nothing leads to physical and emotional atrophy, but creatively challenging yourself benefits your mind and spirit the way exercise benefits your body. It's what keeps you alive.

Procrastination is really a form of trying to live risk-free. It's based on fear of failure. After all, who wouldn't want to put off failure until tomorrow? Besides, by tomorrow or next week or next month maybe something will change. Maybe that big break will just magically materialize, and you won't have to do anything after all.

Maybe it will. But my advice is: Don't count on it.

Evaluating Your Motivators

Albert Einstein was often asked what enabled him to make his revolutionary discoveries. "It's not that I am more gifted than anybody else," he once said. "I'm just more curious than the average person, and I don't give up on a problem until I've found the proper solution. Solving problems is one of my greatest satisfactions in life—and the harder they are, the more satisfaction I get from them."

Einstein's work, then, was its own reward. The benefit was built into the task, entirely independent of any external factors. Is this how you feel about what's happening in your life? What is your motivation for reaching your goals? What are the real benefits of achieving them?

The best motivation is an inner force that inspires you to solve a problem, fill a need, or do something truly excellent. This is known as an *intrinsic* motivator. It's the same force that makes a kid want to ride a bike around the block, just for the fun of it. There are also *extrinsic* motivations, of which money is a prime example. Money should be seen as a byproduct of accomplishment, not as a goal in itself.

Within the two realms of intrinsic and extrinsic motivation, behavior research has identified six forces that can motivate people to achievement:

1. Status with authority figures: Doing something to gain the respect of experts or supervisors.
2. Status with peers: Doing something so that others will look up to you.
3. Acquisitiveness: Wanting to own something so much that you'll do anything to get it.
4. Competitiveness: Desiring to do something so that you can do it bigger and better than anyone else.
5. Concern for excellence: Constantly working at something to make it the best it can possibly be.
6. Achievement via independence: Mastering something for the sake of having the freedom to do it on your own terms.

SELF-QUIZ #1

1. Look over the six categories of achievement motivation. Right now, which ones are motivating you most strongly in your work and in your personal life?

2. In the last five years, has your motivation changed? What do you expect will motivate you ten years from today?

3. Look again at the six types of achievement motivation. Which two are intrinsic? These have proved to be the most effective in helping people achieve their long-range goals. Are these two factors more important to you than the others? In what way?

4. In order to increase concern for excellence as a motivating force in your life, list five things you would take pride in doing to the very best of your ability.

a.

b.

c.

d.

e.

5. Think of one important goal you have in your life today. How do each of the six motivating forces apply to this goal?

    a. Status with experts

    b. Status with peers

    c. Acquisitiveness

    d. Competitiveness

    e. Concern for excellence

    f. Achievement via independence

The Advantages of Incorporating Yourself

As you prepare to embrace risk, start thinking of yourself as a company with a single employee—you! Today, YOU, INC., may contract its services to XYZ Corporation; tomorrow it's likely to sell its services to a different organization. This doesn't mean that you'll be any less loyal to your present employer, but it does mean that you never confuse your personal long-term interests with your current job.

Just as companies must "reinvent" themselves to meet the demands of a changing marketplace, so it is with YOU, INC. Establish your own strategic planning department. Set up your own training department and make sure your prized employee is updating his or her skills and techniques. Start your own pension plan, too.

At the beginning of this chapter, we talked about the growing possibility that you'll be dislocated. The flip side of the coin is that you can choose to dislocate yourself. Today, when the typical American may have several careers in his or her lifetime, an independent, "self-employed" mind-set is essential. If you are not already planning for an eventual career change, you should be.

In leading-edge companies such as Compaq Computer, Levi Strauss, and Xerox, there are no narrowly defined job descriptions. Managers are able to determine what their employees are working on at a given moment and shift them around to various projects as needed. *Freedom* and *flexibility*—not *bureaucracy*—are the operative words. This type of structure lends itself to rapidly changing markets like telecommunications or fashion, where the pace is nonstop. Employees are required to learn new skills and broaden their horizons.

If you don't work for a company that subscribes to this type of management philosophy, you can initiate it on your own. Volunteer to do projects outside your realm of expertise. If you can't spare the time, maybe there's a way to watch others do their jobs in an unobtrusive manner. The more exposure you have, the more skills you develop.

Remember: In the age of chaos, flexibility is the key.

SKILL-BUILDING RECORD

Skills I already have:

Skills I would like to attain:

Steps to be taken (with dates!):

The Power of Patience, and the DOT Principle

Whenever you accept risks, prepare to be criticized and sec-
ond-guessed. This reaction may come from members of your
own profession. It may come from your own company. It may
come from the media. It may even come from your own family
and friends. Expect it—but don't let it stop you.

As you size up resistance to your goals, anticipate where the heat will come from and be flexible in overcoming objections to your approach. You must be prepared to sell your plans and objectives to an indifferent world. Don't simply assume that people will be excited and motivated by your ideas. They won't be unless the idea solves *their* problem or creates an opportunity for *them*. And they still won't be unless you sell them on the benefits.

Everyone wants success, but most people lack two very important qualities: persistence and patience. They're like farmers who keep digging up seeds to see how they're doing, never giving them an opportunity to take root. Be willing to wait longer for your goals to bear fruit than you had anticipated. Impatience is a virtue only when it helps sharpen your focus on what you need to succeed.

Years ago, a young mother was about to go out with her husband. As she prepared to feed their baby before they left, the husband became impatient with her daily routine of mashing vegetables through a strainer. Finally, tired of him standing over her with the car keys in one hand and his other hand on the doorknob, she turned the task over to him. And within a few minutes, the strainer, peas, carrots, and bowl ended up in his lap.

As he changed clothes, he reasoned that there must be a better way to prepare baby food and that there must be a lot of other frustrated parents who didn't enjoy the monotony of straining fruit and vegetables three times a day. Soon they began discussing the idea of designing machinery to strain the food in a factory and sell it already prepared.

Fortunately, the father and his dad owned a small canning plant, but it was difficult to sell the older man on the concept. One mistake that harmed a child would destroy a lifetime of what they had built. What about the expense of marketing surveys, developing and financing new machinery, packaging, getting stores to accept the products and getting parents to buy something totally new at a price that would be both affordable and profitable? The risk was enormous. But they went forward because it filled a need they understood firsthand. They had the skills and experience. And the market was so vast that the risk made sense. The potential benefits far outweighed the downside factors.

One year after Dan Gerber dumped the strainer of cooked vegetables in his lap, the Gerber Products Company introduced its first five baby foods to the market. I have used their products to feed six stubborn, selective babies. (Of course, some of the fruits and vegetables have decorated my shirt, jacket, and tie, not to mention my face and hair. Just because it's preprepared doesn't mean the babies are going to love it!)

The point of the story is that very often an idea becomes a goal when we realize it meets a need in our lives. Our motivation to achieve this goal is dependent upon how strong our need is and whether we have the determination, optimism, and toughness to follow our ideas to fruition.

I've come up with a name for the ability to hang in there when the odds are great, the risk is intimidating, and the road is long and uphill. I call it the DOT Principle, an acronym for Determination, Optimism, and Toughness. These three factors are critical to keeping your goals in focus, despite the delays, frustrations, and setbacks along the way. Determination gives you the resolve to keep going in spite of the roadblocks that lie before you. Optimism gives you the energy boost and focuses your sights on reaching your goals, rather than wallowing in your setbacks. Toughness gives you the resilience to keep pressing on, even if your determination and optimism are lagging.

The importance of the DOT Principle isn't limited to business. With the average age of the American population increasing, there's a need for physical activities and psychological qualities that preserve health and happiness. A study by Dr. Caroline B. Thomas identified a combination of positive factors which she listed under the heading "stamina." Stamina is the strength to withstand disease, fatigue, and hardship. It includes a sense of purpose, steadfastness, and a commitment to solve problems. In our DOT Principle, this is called Determination. . . .

Dr. Thomas's word "stamina" also includes an outgoing, warm temperament. These are elements of Optimism. . . .

And "stamina" includes flexibility, adaptability to change, and resiliency to bend with the buffeting winds of chaos and misfortune. This is what I call Toughness. . . .

When you feel at risk, apply the DOT Principle. Ask yourself: Do I have the DOT in the right place and the right quantity? Do I have the Determination, Optimism, and Toughness to see this through to reach my goal?

Flextactic: Use Your Past to Chart Your Future

Making Your Life a Masterpiece

Have you ever heard the story of how Michelangelo created his statue of David? Legend has it that the block of marble he used had been deemed too long and narrow by other sculptors, and it had stood unused for nearly forty years. But in 1501, Michelangelo saw something the others had missed. He had been commissioned to create a sculpture of David to symbolize the spirit of the city of Florence, and in his mind's eye he created a vision of the figure that this imperfect stone would eventually yield to his hands.

Once Michelangelo had the vision, he began the painstaking process of turning it into reality. He sketched the still-imaginary figure from every angle, then finally began the actual carving. Focusing his vision, he patiently chipped away at the stone until the formless mass gradually became a work of heroic beauty, grace, and wonder.

Asked how he possibly could have wrought such magnificent art from imperfect raw material, Michelangelo replied that the David was *already* inside the block of marble. As an artist, his task had been merely to uncover the finished piece.

Your life is like that stone. Regardless of what anyone has

told you about yourself and your capabilities, you can call upon your inner vision to recognize what others may have been unable to see. By chipping away the rough edges of yourself and getting rid of the unnecessary material, you can create a real masterpiece.

This chipping away can be an ongoing process of self-discovery and accomplishment in every area of your life. Unlike Michelangelo, who had only one opportunity to sculpt that huge block of marble, you have many opportunities to create a life that matches the goals you've set for yourself. Too often we carry dreams within us for years and years, longing for the happiness we would experience "if only" we could make one of those dreams come true. Like that block of marble—ignored, unvalued, and unused—we allow our talents, our hopes, and our dreams to lie lifeless within us.

In every moment of our lives we program (or allow others to program) our positive or negative self-concepts. These images of ourselves are in many ways like the automatic pilot of a jet aircraft: They are programs without a value-judging function. They simply strive to fulfill the attitudes and beliefs we've set for them, and they don't care whether they are positive or negative, true or false, right or wrong, safe or dangerous. Their only capability is to follow previous instructions, implicitly and automatically.

How important are your hopes and dreams to your internal guidance system? Have you made them secondary to the effects of the negative experiences that everyone must inevitably endure, or do you give your personal vision the supreme importance that it deserves? Do you think of your goals as one-of-a-kind sculptures to be revealed and cherished, or as silly musings that aren't worthy of your attention?

Most important, are your goals flexible enough to survive the constantly changing environment we live in? What happens when you suddenly have to plot a new course? Are you able to adjust when long-held beliefs about who you are and where you're headed seem to vanish before your eyes? Are you able to successfully handle the moments of sudden transition that are sure to occur?

At moments of sudden transition you are experiencing *chaos,* which you now know is perfectly natural and brimming with opportunity. These chaotic moments may happen every two years or every ten, but the chances are you'll be called upon to change course with greater frequency than you ever imagined, perhaps having several careers in one lifetime. Though frequent change may be commonplace today, it is never easy; true change always comes with some sense of discomfort. When it happens, you must be ready to meet the challenge and to seize the opportunity.

The Search for Self-definition: Four Basic Questions

In the goal-achievement seminars I conduct all over the world, I always suggest that participants go for a walk by themselves and answer four basic questions. I describe this as a time of solitude and reflection, but many people find that the answers to these questions are long-held beliefs that have simply never been admitted or recognized.

The first question is: "If it weren't for money, time, and personal responsibilities, what would I really love to do with my life? In other words, if I were free to do whatever I wanted, what would I begin doing tomorrow morning?"

That's a big question, all right. The other three questions can help to clarify your response. Here they are:

- What did you love to do as a child? What were you really good at? What made you feel proud?
- What makes you feel that way now?
- Are you doing something to benefit other people? Does that give you a feeling of self-respect and fulfillment?

You may wonder how revisiting your childhood can help you chart your goals. A remarkable series of films made in England over a twenty-eight-year period disclosed that what we love and do well as children continues to be our real talent as adults. The filmmakers tracked the lives of fifty people, beginning at age seven and with reevaluations occurring every seven years until the age of thirty-five.

Surprisingly, nearly all the subjects eventually found work that was related to interests they had already demonstrated between the ages of seven and fourteen. Although most of them had discarded or strayed from those interests in early adulthood, virtually all found their way back to their childhood dreams by age thirty-five.

Can you remember what you really wanted to be as a child? When I was a young boy I had a recurring fantasy of standing in a beautiful theater like Lincoln Center or Radio City Music Hall in New York. I was wearing a tuxedo, and I was bowing to an appreciative audience after some kind of performance, with my mother, father, sister, brother, and grandparents smiling in the front row. This vision began when I was nine and continued for many years . . . until I found myself, not too long ago, in a tuxedo, speaking to an audience in Carnegie Hall in New York. My parents and family weren't in the front row, as they had been in my fantasy, but everything else about the setting was nearly identical!

As a boy growing up in London, young Andrew Lloyd Webber loved to attend matinee performances of musicals. Soon he was writing his own shows and producing them at home in a model theater that he built himself. It even had a revolving stage, made from the turntable of an old record player. Years later, he read some poems by T. S. Eliot on a plane flight from London to Los Angeles. An unlikely idea struck him: Why not create a musical based on some of Eliot's poems? Though it seemed like a great idea to Andrew, most potential backers did not agree. T. S. Eliot's poems just didn't seem like the kind of book a successful entrepreneur reads on an airplane, and his name certainly didn't seem like one that would bring crowds flocking to a theater. Eventually, Andrew Lloyd Webber had to take out a mortgage on his home to help pay for the production—and of course *Cats* went on to be the most profitable musical of all time.

When she was a young girl growing up in Detroit, Diana Ross used to tag along on weekends when her mother worked at extra jobs to support her family. One such job took place on Saturday mornings: Diana's mother cleaned out a movie theater with the aid of a huge, noisy blower. Each seat had to be blown free of popcorn husks and candy wrappers, and then the floor underneath had to be attacked as well. It was a long, tough job, and at the end there would always be a huge mound of debris at the front of the theater, waiting to be hauled out to the garbage cans in the alley. And by this time the projectionist would also have arrived. The day's first movie was almost always flickering across the screen before the piles of plastic cups and cardboard boxes had been cleared away.

For most kids, this would not have seemed like a very glamorous experience. But as Diana watched her mom and helped as much as she could, the vacant movie theater was charged with excitement and high expectation. There was going to be a movie, and Diana would get to see it—or at least part of it—absolutely free! Once that happened, nothing else mattered. Whether it was a Western or a war movie, whether the story was set in ancient Egypt or on the planet Mars, whether the actors were white (almost always), black (very rarely), or purple (almost never!), Diana lost herself in the flickering images on the screen. She was a star already. The world just didn't know it yet—but the world was going to find out.

As a boy in Scottsdale, Arizona, Steven Spielberg liked to shoot 8-mm films featuring "ordinary people pursued by large forces." He was his own writer, director, and star—and he knew that this was what he wanted to do for the rest of his life, albeit on a larger scale. There seemed to be no point in going to college. Movies, after all, were made in Hollywood, so that's where Steven went. Dressed in a suit, carrying a briefcase, and looking like he belonged, he would sneak past the guards at the entrances to the major studio lots and then spend the day just walking around, soaking up the atmosphere. Eventually one of his short films gained some attention—and today, of course, Steven Spielberg has directed not just one but half a dozen of the most profitable films ever.

If you've lost track of a goal that was once your vision of the future, explore what it would take to begin pursuing that goal at this point in your life. If you're not sure what the goal is, look over the four questions above. By answering them, you can give the future a new clarity and purpose. By at last projecting your childhood dreams out into the world, you can begin to be who you *want* to be.

Use your past to focus on your Life-Forming Goals for the future. Of course, the goals you hold now don't have to be the same ones you had when you were twelve years old, but, as we've seen, there usually is some relationship between our childhood dreams and what we (secretly?) want as adults.

Take some time to think about all this, because now you're about to do something very important. I'm going to ask you to begin keeping a journal of your progress toward all your goals. In my opinion, a journal is simply the single most powerful tool you can use for achieving your objectives in life.

Of course, before you can begin working with this powerful tool, you'll need a book that will serve as your journal. Right now is a good time to go out and get that book—before you read any farther. Leather-bound journals (and less elegant but perfectly serviceable blank-page books) are available at most bookstores. I suggest you choose one carefully, just as you might choose a companion for a long and exciting voyage of discovery. You may be using this book for many years, and even after it's filled up you'll surely want it indefinitely, to look back on the challenges you faced and the strategies you devised to meet them.

When you've acquired your journal and have it open in front of you, you're ready to perform what I consider one of the most momentous acts anyone can undertake. On the first page of your journal, you're going to write down your Life-Forming Goals.

Before you do so, remember that these Life-Forming Goals should be general enough to absorb the unexpected changes that are going to occur over the years, but also specific enough to be more than merely vague daydreams. If you want to be a great brain surgeon, don't just say you'll be a doctor. But don't feel that you have to be especially rigid about all the details as you write your Life-Forming Goals.

I personally believe that the number of Life-Forming Goals should be very limited. You should have no more than three or four of them in each of two categories: Professional Goals and Personal Goals. To some extent the two categories will inevitably overlap. If one of your Personal Goals is to travel to Africa to climb Mount Kilimanjaro, you will probably have to achieve a certain level of professional success in order to afford the trip. But if you're thinking clearly about what you really want from life, you should be able to intuitively make the distinction between Personal and Professional Goals.

Focus Plus Flexibility

When you've written your Life-Forming Goals on page 1 of your journal, turn the page and get ready to define the intervening steps that will realize those dreams.

To keep focused but flexible, I've learned to envision the road to my Life-Forming Goals in terms of three time frames, which I call Long-term Goals, Intermediate Goals, and Immediate Goals.

I anticipate that Long-term Goals will take more than three years to accomplish. They include overall career, family, and financial plans, as well as things I intend to do or be in later years. Intermediate Goals require six months to three years. Purchasing a new home or getting a postgraduate degree are typical of these kinds of objectives. Lastly, there are Immediate Goals, which can be achieved within the next three to six months.

Immediate Goals should be further broken down into component subgoals. For example, I recently set an Immediate Goal of acquiring more advanced computer skills. I wrote this goal in my journal and then began to break it down as follows:

1. Identify the required skills.
   a. Discuss skills with mentors and experts in my industry.
   b. Read about trends in the computer industry and anticipate new programs.
   c. Consult computer publications and attend trade shows.
2. Find a course of study that teaches these skills quickly and affordably.
   a. Call local college or vocational center.

    b. Consult knowledgeable computer software salesperson about instructional programs.

3. Attend and complete such a course.
4. Seek immediate opportunities to implement new skills for maximum reinforcement of learning.

To see how this process works, let's return to Jeff Sampson, the engineer we discussed at the very beginning of this book. Jeff had had his sights set on becoming a top executive at his large aerospace company, but the firm suddenly began downsizing. Jeff had been working on improving his visibility within the company by initiating new ideas and by increasing his productivity. As part of his Immediate Goals, he had been taking business classes at a local college and hoped to receive a credential that would attract the attention of upper management. For his Intermediate Goals, Jeff hoped to improve the performance of the employees he currently supervised, and to become the head of his department relatively soon. All this was moving him toward his Life Goal of being at or near the top of the whole company. Abruptly losing his job was an obstacle for Jeff—but starting his own firm was the opportunity he discovered. Although the new venture required him to completely restructure his goals, he was able to create new and even more exciting objectives for his life and career.

There's just one more thing. When you're writing in your journal about any of your goals, don't use phrases like "I hope to be this" or "I want to do that."

Instead, write *"I am becoming . . ."* and *"I am doing . . ."*

Because you are becoming! And you are doing what's important to succeed!

CHAPTER FOUR

Flextactic: Make Your Life an Open Book

Who Are You . . . Really?

When you've written your Life-Forming Goals on the first page of your journal and your Intermediate Goals on the second, you'll be able to revisit them whenever you make a new entry, and I hope you'll open your journal and write in it every day. As time passes, you'll be amazed at how much this one book can teach you about yourself.

But let me clarify exactly what I think a journal should be. I don't think, for example, that a journal should be a diary.

A diary is like a personal album made up of word pictures. Writing in it and looking back over what you've written can be very useful, a lot of fun, and sometimes a bit scary. A diary shows where you've been physically, and who you were emotionally and psychologically. Perhaps it shows you at the company picnic wearing wing tips and plaid Bermuda shorts!

A diary is a record of what has already happened in your life, and a journal can include some of that information too. But a journal is really a projection of *what you are going to make happen*. It is not just a look back at your personal history; it is a look forward in time at the personal story you are determined to create.

I began my own journal by writing a detailed description of myself as I was at the start of my goal-achievement program.

Every day since then I've added new ideas, new concepts, and new suggestions. When I'm writing, I try to think of myself as an artist painting the future. At first the changes I chose to make in my life were subtle, like brush strokes creating shading and light. But over time the portrait has taken on a vivid character. Yesterday's dreams have become today's realities.

Before you can visualize the person you really want to become, you'll need a sense of where you've been in the past, where you are today, and the various kinds of resources that are available to you. All this can be accomplished by compiling a personal inventory, which will be the first entry in your journal.

There is power in putting this information on paper. Once again, you'll find yourself thinking back through your life to identify the unique qualities that only you possess. As you do so, you'll discover important bits of information about yourself. Like atoms or cells, these bits of information can form bonds and alliances with one another to create greater and more exciting possibilities in all areas of your life.

In her book *Leadership and the New Science,* Margaret Wheatley says that looking closely at an apparently chaotic system always reveals its latent order. Wheatley writes, "Even the most chaotic systems never go beyond certain boundaries; they stay contained within a shape that we can define as the system's strange attractor." Strange attractors may sound like something out of a science fiction/love story, but in the terminology of the new physics they are unique shapes made up of what might have seemed like millions of completely random particles or space-time events. Strange attractors can help us understand that there is a pattern to be found even amid the turbulence of our lives, and your journal can help you focus on and visualize the "strange attractor" in your life. The journal is your private crystal ball that swirls the elements of your past and present to shape a vision of your future.

First, begin your journal's personal inventory by identifying your greatest character strengths. Although your journal is "for your eyes only" and should not be shared with anyone, I will share with you a few inventory items I jotted down regarding my own character. I started with "caring" and "trustworthy." I also added "joyful," "creative," "optimistic," and "good communicator." You, on the other hand, might have a natural ability to lead others. Do people enjoy being with you? Are you inquisitive and curious about the world around you? Are you always willing and eager to lend a helping hand? You should list at least five character traits that you perceive as your major strengths.

Second, identify your natural talents and abilities, emphasizing what you feel you were born with or have exhibited throughout your life. Do you have a strong physical constitution? Do you have the capability to endure hard physical work? Are you artistic? Do you have musical talent? Are you good with words? Are you highly intuitive? Do you have good mechanical or mathematical ability? Are you highly creative?

Third, write down any educational and training experiences that have resulted in special knowledge and skills. What degrees do you hold? What special seminars and courses have you taken? What have you read about and studied? Have you worked alongside a parent, other relative, or friend in a business or profession in a role that has functioned as an apprenticeship in that field? Be sure to include areas of self-study. This is not like a résumé for a specific job. These journal entries are to help you design your future.

Fourth, list the individuals who form your primary personal and professional network. I classify these people as either "sounding boards" or "springboards." A "sounding board" is someone with good judgment, who can listen to your ideas and from whom you can get practical, helpful feedback. A "springboard" is a person with influence, who can elevate your level of contacts by introduction and referral. Both categories can include co-workers, former classmates, business contacts, family members, and friends. They don't even necessarily have to be people you've actually met, as long as they're important to you intellectually and emotionally.

No one achieves success in a vacuum, and you should make a conscious effort to ally yourself with individuals who share your values and your goals. As the owner of the new Toronto Raptors in the National Basketball Association, John Bitove was determined to find an aggressive, risk-taking general manager for the team, because this was Bitove's own personality. After all, founding a professional basketball team in a city that's historically oriented toward hockey in the wintertime isn't exactly a conservative move. Bitove could have had his pick of seasoned administrators to lead his new team, but instead he chose thirty-four-year-old Isiah Thomas, who had been a championship player in the league but who had absolutely no management experience whatsoever. Above all, however, Bitove wanted someone who shared his go-for-broke philosophy. And as the Toronto team began its first season, few could find fault with the owner or his choice of Isiah Thomas: The Raptors were the first expansion team in the history of the NBA to win their opening regular season game.[5]

Unlike sounding boards, who are often longtime personal friends, springboard relationships can be your conscious creations. Don't feel the slightest bit uneasy about this. If there's someone you admire—someone who has arrived at the point in his or her career that you're still shooting for—make an effort to seek that person out and introduce yourself. You don't have to be pushy about it, and a politely written letter that succinctly outlines some of your ideas will often draw a genuinely interested response. Successful people like meeting with those on the way up in their chosen field. And successful people know how to distinguish the real comers from the phonies. If you're a sincerely motivated, goal-directed winner, the leaders in your field will be glad to know you. They'll very willingly become springboards to your growing list of achievements.

The final entry in this personal inventory section of your journal should list your mentors and role models. Once again, these may be relatives or close friends, but they're just as likely to be people whom you've never met. The only hard-and-fast requirement is that the lives and accomplishments of your role models must inspire you to do your very best.

My mentor and role model is someone I've only read about and heard about from my teachers: Benjamin Franklin. Through his example, I've learned to expect a great deal more from myself, realizing that it is never too late to become inventive and imaginative. When I go to the library to read or borrow a wonderful book, I think of him. He founded America's first library at the age of twenty-five. When I mail a letter, I am reminded that he founded the U.S. Mail at the age of thirty-one. When I hear the siren of a fire engine, heading for yet another California brushfire, I thank him, silently, because he started the first fire department, also at the age of thirty-one.

When I put some kindling wood in our old pot-bellied stove on a crisp evening in our mountain retreat, I am warmed by the fact that he designed it when he was thirty-six years old. When I flip the on-switch and my personal computer hums into action, I am grateful that he harnessed electricity at the age of forty. Lightning hit our barn recently and knocked out our electricity and phone service for two days. The barn survived, thanks to the lightning rod he invented at age forty-three. Several of my kids just had to go east and get a real education at the Ivy League university he founded at age forty-five. And when I try to read the menu in the ambiance of an intimate, candle-lit French restaurant, I sigh with the realization of advancing age and reach for my bifocals, which he invented at age seventy-nine.

With just two years of formal schooling, he was an international wit, conversationalist, economist, philosopher, diplomat, inventor, statesman, printer, publisher, and linguist who spoke and wrote five languages. He even conceived the idea of paratroopers from balloons, more than a century before the airplane was invented. I've had eighteen years of formal education, cramming me full of more pure knowledge than Benjamin Franklin ever had at my age. He expected a great deal of himself and lived every day looking for more problems to solve, more mysteries to understand, and more questions to ask for eighty-four highly motivated years.

SAMPLE JOURNAL PAGES

Personal Character Strengths

1.

2.

3.

4.

5.

6.

7.

Natural Talents and Abilities

1.

2.

3.

4.

5.

6.

7.

Educational Background (include degrees attained, classes, seminars, courses)

Areas of Informal Study (reading, research, writing)

Special Knowledge or Skills

Personal and Professional Network

Sounding Boards and Springboards

Mentors and Role Models

What Is the Future Made Of?

Once you've completed the personal inventory section of your journal, the focus shifts away from the past. My good friend and colleague Zig Ziglar tells of some insights he gained from Walter Hailey, who built a successful life-insurance business that was eventually sold to Kmart for $78 million. As a sales professional, Hailey had the opportunity to meet and get to know thousands of people over the course of his long career. Unfortunately, many of these individuals were not where they had hoped to be either personally or professionally, and Hailey gradually began to see exactly how this had come to pass. Most people, he realized, are almost constantly looking back in anger at the events of their lives—and when they're not looking back in anger, they're looking ahead in fear. The result, of course, is frustration and emotional paralysis. And those are definitely not to be included in your list of Life-Forming Goals!

On the first blank page of your journal following the personal inventory section, write your Life-Forming Goals again, and then read them out loud. Remember, you should read them every day as you prepare to make a new entry in the journal, and from time to time you should write them as well.

Always begin each entry on a fresh page, and at the top of the page write the subgoal that you're interested in accomplishing *that day*. The rest of the entry should be a description—just like a movie preview—of how you want the day's events to unfold. This is somewhat similar to the visualization techniques we'll be taking up in the next chapter, but here our focus is very specific and short-term. You are simply showing how the achievement of your subgoal is going to happen that very day. Write it in the present tense because that's the best way to actually see events unfold in your mind's eye: ''I close the biggest deal of my life'' is much more effective psychologically than ''I am going to close the biggest deal'' or ''I want to close the biggest deal.''

Don't worry about the details—except the really exciting ones! For example, as you create a word preview of a spectacularly effective presentation you're going to make that afternoon, don't feel that you have to describe how you'll look for a space in your client's parking lot. Just hit the high notes: how confident you feel as you talk with the client, and how you sense from the beginning that things are going well. Try to ''see'' this as clearly as possible: How would the client's enthusiasm be revealed? Would he or she be leaning forward, listening carefully to every word? Would he or she suddenly ask your permission to bring another decision maker into the office to hear about the exciting business opportunity you're offering? Would you actually walk out the door with a check to cover your first order?

Page after page of your journal should be filled with these ''movie previews'' of the Oscar-winning film that will be your life. And if things don't always work out exactly as shown in the ''preview,'' don't allow yourself to get discouraged. The intention of the journal is not to test the accuracy with which you can predict the future. Rather, the journal's purpose is to create a positive vision of goal achievement which will imprint itself on your subconscious mind as a positive *expectation* of success. This is tremendously important and beneficial. In fact, studies have shown that positive expectations are the most important factors in virtually all enterprises, whether it's hitting a serve or serving a customer.

Realistically, you can't control the million and one variables that are brought to bear on any event. But you can *always* control your responses and your expectations. Your journal can be an all-important tool to help you exercise that control. By writing your way through the scenes you want to see in your life, you can take a giant step toward creating the future you want to have.

Remember what you learned about Michelangelo at the beginning of the last chapter. Where others saw only a block of imperfect marble, Michelangelo "saw" the completed statue of David before he even picked up hammer and chisel. What do *you* see as you look at a blank page of your journal?

More often than you might think, what you see is what you'll get!

CHAPTER FIVE

Flextactic: Use the Power of Visualization

Turning Thought into Reality: It's Easier Than You Think

I've always been fascinated by reports of patients undergoing brain surgery who have reexperienced sensations from their past as various areas of the brain were stimulated. The patients' recall was so vivid: sounds, colors, conversations, and dozens of other details reappeared with astonishing accuracy. These people were reliving the past, not just remembering it.

Just as we can relive our memories, we also have the capability to "prelive" experiences that we want to happen in the future. In fact, that's the whole purpose of goal setting. By visualizing your goals, you can preview your life's coming attractions. This can dramatically enhance your motivation for making those goals come true.

As you make entries in your journal, you are creating written previews of situations in which you successfully achieve the subgoals that eventually compose your life-forming accomplishments. But with the visualization techniques we'll discuss in this chapter, you'll be focusing more on final, long-term results than on the immediate, "tactical" situations represented by subgoals. In other words, you'll be visualizing your life as it will be when your life-forming goals have actually been achieved.

Visualization requires active use of your imagination, but

there's nothing difficult or esoteric about it. In fact, you already know how to create vivid mental images that can affect not only your moods but the workings of your physical body as well. To prove this, close your eyes and imagine that you are slicing a juicy lemon with a sharp knife. Try to "see" this action as clearly as possible: the yellow skin of the lemon, the feel of the knife cutting through it, and the juice spilling out. Then, with your eyes still closed, imagine you are picking up a piece of the lemon and placing it on your tongue. Even though this entire sequence is taking place only in your imagination, your mouth will begin to salivate. Your body "believes" that you are actually eating a lemon.

Can these visualization techniques have practical benefits? Very definitely! In an experiment to test kinesthetic learning skills, two equally athletic groups of youngsters in a high school gym class were given basic instructions in shooting basketball free throws. Afterward, both groups were allowed to practice for two weeks—but while one group could practice by actually executing free throws with a real basketball, the second group could only *imagine* doing so. The second group's free throws were to be "shot" only in their minds, by visualizing one perfect toss after another. At the end of two weeks, the group that had been practicing with a real ball and baskets showed obvious improvement. But so did the second group, who had only been visualizing success. In fact, the improvement in the second group's performance was every bit as great as the first group's.

Through the power of visualization, you too can benefit from the scientifically proven knowledge that imagination leads to goal achievement. The first step is realizing that your imagination is much more than a mere vestige of your childhood, or something that you either have or don't have. Rather, your imagination is an important success-building skill that you need to cultivate.

Here are a few preliminary exercises to stimulate the power

of your creative imagination. By using them from time to time throughout the day, you'll build up your mental capacity for guided imagery just as jogging regularly builds up your cardio-vascular system:

1. Become acutely aware of sensory feedback. Take in as many sights, sounds, smells, textures, and tastes as you can. If you're at the beach, take a moment to close your eyes and feel the texture of the wet sand under your feet. Smell the sea breeze and listen with focused attention to the roar of the surf. Later, try to mentally reexperience those sensations as vividly as you can. Of course, you can perform similar exercises wherever you happen to be. The main thing is to become more aware of your environment.

2. As you listen to people talking at business or social gatherings, try to form mental images of what's being said. Even if what's being said is about as interesting as watching paint dry, you can make good use of the situation by turning it into a practice session for improving your imaging skills.

3. When you're the one who's speaking, use words that are rich in visual imagery. Make a conscious effort to describe events and plans in great detail, and with more enthusiasm than is your normal style. This will also help you become a better conversationalist and public speaker.

4. This simple technique is useful in any setting. I've found it to be especially useful on airplanes or in airports while waiting for a flight. Begin by sitting comfortably in a chair. Relax for a few seconds and look at the people and objects around you. Then, with your eyes closed, try to recall as many sights as you can. You may be surprised at the number of things you fail to remember.

Make an effort to repeat this exercise at least once a day in different settings.

5. Close your eyes and hold an object in your hand. Feel the object as you move it from one hand to the other. Trace the shape of the object with your fingers and picture its shape at the same time in your mind. As a variation of this exercise, use an imaginary object instead of a real one. Pretend that you've got an ice cube in your right hand. Feel your skin becoming cold and the moisture dripping between your fingers as the cube begins to melt.

The late Glenn Gould was one of the most gifted pianists of the century—and one of the most eccentric. Much to the dismay of the concertgoing public, Gould all but gave up live performances in order to devote himself to creating perfect recordings of important pieces of music from the classical repertoire. Gould had an astonishing ability to negotiate even the most difficult passages, and he did so using his well-developed powers of visualization. With his eyes closed as he sat at the piano, he would actually "see" himself playing as if he were watching from across the room. By seeing himself give a perfect rendition of the music, he was able to produce one in real life.

On one occasion, Glenn Gould had to make a recording on a piano that was not up to his exacting standards. Though he was notoriously temperamental, the recording session with full orchestral accompaniment could not be rescheduled. Gould went into a room by himself, closed his eyes, and visualized the best piano he had ever played. He recalled every sensation associated with playing that wonderful piano: the action of the keys, the full sound of the notes, even the kind of chair he'd been sitting on. Then he returned to the studio and completed the recording session on the second-rate instrument. But he was no longer playing that instrument; in his own mind, he was continuing to

visualize the best piano he had ever played. Listeners were aston-
ished, and many felt it was the best performance Gould had ever
given.

Learning to sharpen your imagination is well worth the effort. It can help you join the goal-oriented achievers who use
their thoughts as a personal video library of future success.

Visualizing the Person You Want to Become

I'll never forget what the great Russian sprinter and Olympic gold medalist Valeri Borzov told me in an interview about
his approach to the hundred-meter-sprint finals. Borzov said,
"By learning to draw a mental picture of the race while I was
still in the starting blocks, I was able to react to the starting gun
with split-second speed. And when the shot was fired, my inner
computer—programmed to get me out of the motionless state—
switched on and took over, projecting me forward about ten me-
ters ahead of where I was actually running."

In my work with Olympic athletes and NASA astronauts,
we used a technique known as VMBR, or Visual Motor Behavior
Rehearsal. Because of the direct relationship between visualization and actual performance, we taught the Olympians and astronauts to be masters in the art of simulation.

For a vivid example of how simulation works, you might
visit a NASA center or an airline-pilot training facility. One such
facility, operated by American Airlines in Dallas, is open for
public tours. There, pilots use interactive video and computer
technology to "fly" the simulator through every type of weather
condition and emergency. They taxi from the ramp, take off, fly
to a city, and land—never leaving the ground but experiencing
nearly every physical and emotional sensation that could be en-

countered on an actual flight. In the same way, trial lawyers and sales representatives simulate success by going through their presentations in front of peers in settings that are as realistic as possible.

Simulation allows you to perform a task and get it right, but without the pressure created by fear of failure. Then, when you face the real thing—when you're called upon for actual high-performance achievement—it will be almost like repeating a simulation drill.

My studies of high achievers have shown me that no matter how different their personalities, their work habits, or their occupations, the people who accomplish great things in life have visualized and expected success all along. They've had the ability to vividly picture their achievements and to reassure themselves in the face of long odds that they would come through.

To visualize the person you want most to become, set aside some time in which you can create an atmosphere that's conducive to identifying your life dreams. I like to go to the loft in my barn in the mountains for this. I might take a long drive by the ocean, or a walk in the woods or park. Or I might just sit quietly in a comfortable chair.

Get yourself in the mood for visualizing. When the left hemisphere of the brain is quiet and relaxed, the mind is most receptive to creative inputs. To facilitate this, I use recorded music. I love Bach, Handel, Vivaldi, and George Winston, and I have a personal affinity for strings. I also love epic movie theme music like "Last of the Mohicans," "Dances with Wolves," "Somewhere in Time," and "Out of Africa." As I listen to the music, I remember and reflect on the happiest moments of my past. I allow myself to travel back in time and mentally relive those rich experiences.

Once you're in a properly relaxed and optimistic mood, let your mind focus on who you really want to become. Visualize the future in two time frames: five years from now and ten years from now. Of course, these images might have to change with the realities of a chaotic world, but for the purposes of this visualization you can assume that your life will proceed on a smooth, uninterrupted course.

Design a day in your life five years from now. Incredible as it seems, you'll be entering a new century. Keep in mind that many of the world's greatest inventions came at the close of a century, as if humanity felt some urgency to be more creative as one era gave way to the next. Who are you five years from now? Where are you geographically? On Monday mornings, where do you go? What are you doing, seeing, feeling, and thinking? Who are the people around you? What is different about your life?

Now, project ahead ten years from today. Picture a film of your life at that time—not a home video but a wide-screen spectacular in full gleaming color and Dolby sound. Who is watching it with you? What dramatic moments are depicted by that film? What personal triumphs are revealed? What obstacles are courageously overcome?

Don't be shy! The purpose of this exercise is to load visualized software into your mental computer. Just as a computer must be configured to accept specific materials, your mind must be prepared to accept the reality of your success. By introducing positive images of goal achievement, you are preparing yourself to translate those images into reality.

I especially like to visualize myself being introduced at a dinner in my honor. The emcee comes to the microphone and reads the highlights of my career and personal life and adds some personal insights as to who I really am. What would the emcee be saying about you if such a dinner were held in your honor ten years from now? Devote a page of your journal to describing the things you would want said about who you are and what you've done.

Are you on a path now that leads to the future self the

emcee is describing? Or have you settled for a level of aspiration much lower than what is called for by your innermost desires?

It was a stormy night many years ago when an elderly couple entered the hotel lobby and asked for a room. "I'm very sorry," responded the night clerk. "We are completely full with a convention group. Normally, I would send you to another hotel that we use for overflow at times like this, but I can't imagine sending you out into the storm again. Why don't you stay in my room?" the young man offered with a smile. "It may not be a luxury suite, but it's clean. I can finish up some bookkeeping here in the office."

The distinguished-looking man and woman seemed uncomfortable at inconveniencing the clerk, but they graciously accepted his offer. When the gentleman went to pay his bill the next morning, the clerk was still at the desk and said, "Oh, I live here full-time so there's no charge for the room. You don't need to worry about that."

The older man nodded and said to the clerk, "You're the kind of person that every hotel owner dreams about having as an employee. Maybe someday I'll build a hotel for you." The hotel clerk was flattered, but the idea sounded so outrageous that he was sure the man was joking.

A few years passed and the hotel clerk was still at the same job. One day he received a registered letter from the man. The letter expressed his vivid recollections of that stormy night, along with an invitation and a round-trip ticket for the hotel clerk to visit him in New York. Arriving a few days later in Manhattan, the clerk was met by his friend at the corner of Fifth Avenue and Thirty-fourth Street, where a magnificent new building stood. "That," exclaimed the man, "is the hotel I've built for you to run! I told you at the time that it might happen and today you can see that I was serious."

The clerk was stunned. "What's the catch? Why me? Who are you anyway?" he stammered. "My name is William Waldorf Astor. And there is no catch. You are the person I want working for me." That hotel was the original Waldorf-Astoria, and the name of the young clerk who accepted the first managerial position was George C. Boldt.

This is a true story, and there's a personal message in it for all of us. Why do we need a benefactor to come along and make us believe in our dreams? How is it that an outsider can perceive more potential in us than we can sometimes see in ourselves? The purpose of visualization and simulation is to help you "see" all the unlimited opportunities that are yours for the taking.

CHAPTER SIX

Flextactic: Create a Blueprint for Success

From Artist to Artisan

So far in this book I've asked you for the most part to think like an artist: to step back from the canvas of your life and to envision the "big picture" that you're going to create from now on. Now it's time to start thinking in very practical terms, like a craftsman—a carpenter, perhaps, or a stonemason. You've got the materials, and you've got your dream house clearly in mind. You now need a blueprint to help you build a foundation and eight rooms, plus all the features that will define the house as your unique creation.

Beyond question, all the soul-searching and visualizing and journal writing that you've done in the previous chapters puts you far ahead of the majority of the people in the world in many important respects. Indeed, less than 5 percent of the U.S. population ever read a nonfiction book or listen to an educational program after their basic schooling is completed. And less than 5 percent of the population will ever write down a goal they want to achieve. By failing to plan, all these people are actually planning to fail.

Many people take more care in planning their vacations than they devote to thinking about the important issues of their lives. As they eagerly look forward to the break from reality that a vacation represents, they become deeply involved in selecting a destination, setting a date, buying tickets, calculating a budget, and arranging all the details of the trip from dog kennels to plant-watering house sitters—yet they almost never approach life's bigger agenda with the same degree of thought and preparation.

Several years ago a study was commissioned by the U.S. Department of Labor to examine links between formal education and real-world skills. The final report defined three categories of ability—Basic Skills, Thinking Skills, and Personal Qualities—that are fundamental to success in the workplace. Then the report took note of an interesting fact: In two of the three categories, goal setting is highly important. As a component of Thinking Skills, for example, goal setting forces us to recognize risks, to generate alternatives, and to identify the best alternatives. Goals are also important in the Personal Qualities category by fostering accurate self-assessment and the development of self-control.

In today's chaotic and fast-changing world, the information in this Department of Labor report becomes especially significant. Personal qualities such as flexibility, adaptability, and careful identification of objectives are now key requirements for success. Without these qualities, the report warns, one's chances for survival in an increasingly competitive business environment become extremely precarious, to say the least.

In order to achieve prosperity and fulfillment now and in the years ahead, you simply must begin planning your future with as much care as you would prepare for a round-the-world trip by air and ground transportation. What's more, your plans must be flexible enough to allow for some detours, some side trips, and even the possibility that you may completely lose track of the road you started on. Instead of seeing this as a catastrophe, you must discover how the new road can still get you exactly where you want to go.

Goals and the Art of Juggling

When was the last time you went to a circus? Unfortunately, many people haven't gone since they were very young—but maybe that's why we have grandchildren: They give us a reason to become childlike again. When I gather my grandchildren and take them to the circus in San Diego, I always try to get front-row seats so we can get a close look at the performers. I think it's because they remind me of myself. They've devoted their lives to developing certain skills, and they travel from city to city performing for the benefit of others, as I travel nearly every day lecturing to corporations about individual and team achievement.

Jugglers have always especially fascinated me. I find myself wondering if they practiced juggling as kids while the rest of us were learning to throw and catch just one ball. One night at the circus, while the juggler was throwing eight balls up in the air at once, I suddenly pulled out my notepad and started writing. My wife, Susan, stuck her cotton candy in my face and frowned at me, thinking I was working while she and our grandkids were enjoying the show. But I wasn't working—I was thinking about an analogy between my own life and the life of a juggler. I scribbled these notes, which still have pink cotton-candy stains on them:

In a sense, we are all jugglers. Each day of our lives we juggle our career, homelife, family, friends, creditors, health, hobbies, and peace of mind . . . some of us are better at it than others. But we all have about eight to ten "balls" in the air at any given time. When the circus juggler drops a ball, he lets it bounce and picks it up on the next bounce, without losing his rhythm or concentration. He keeps right on juggling. Many times we do the same thing. We lose our jobs, but get another one on the first or second bounce. We may drop the ball on a sale, on an opportunity to move ahead, or in a relationship. We've got to pick up that ball on the rebound or get a new one thrown in to replace what we've just dropped.

Some of the balls—or priorities—that we juggle just won't bounce. They're as fragile as fine crystal, and if we drop them, they break. What are the delicate priorities that you're juggling in your life? Are any of them labeled "loved ones" or "health" or "moral character"? For a long time one of my problems was that the priorities I was most attentive to were "rubber balls" such as deadlines and work schedules. I didn't realize that these had much more elasticity than precious, irreplaceable responsibilities like family, health, integrity, and life-long relationships.

Right now, read over the life-forming goals you entered in your journal. Then, beside each one, list all the benefits you'll gain when the goal has been achieved. Be detailed, be vivid, make the benefits real for you. Keep in mind the importance of concentrating or focusing your energy, like a laser beam.

As a child, I discovered this principle on my own by experimenting with sunlight and a magnifying glass. The more concentrated that little bright dot of sunlight became, the more powerful the result. I could literally set paper on fire! When you concentrate on benefits, you ignite the flame of desire that's the energy behind every positive achievement.

By listing the benefits of reaching your goals, you can begin to arrange them in their true order of importance. You may be surprised to realize that certain of your goals are more important to you than others. By prioritizing your goals, you can give them proper balance as you juggle them within the constraints of time. Handle your priorities with care. Some of them just don't bounce!

In my opinion, you should give special emphasis to goals related to health and to relationships with family and loved ones.

63

If you have a health problem that restricts your life in any way, you should probably begin to network with others who have turned disabilities into opportunities. If you shatter a relationship, it's important not to blame the other person; rather, examine your own attitudes and actions. Determining blame is of little use. The key is to determine the cause. And if you find yourself in a career crisis, pick up the pieces by assessing your natural talents, your education, and your unique skills.

"Reality Checking" Your Goals

Once you've listed the benefits of your life-forming goals and prioritized them, a "reality check" is the next step.

Goals must be challenging, but not unrealistic. Can you formulate a practical plan consisting of manageable steps in order to reach a given objective? If the answer is yes, you know you've defined a realistic goal. But if you can't come up with a plan, with every succeeding step building on the previous ones, then your goals aren't realistic in those areas of your life.

Here are some self-check questions to help determine how realistic your goals are:

1. Are you in a position of responsibility for your own achievement? Does success or failure depend primarily on you?

Avoid goals that depend on others or luck to be accomplished. Remember the story about the man who prayed every night to win the lottery: "Dear God, please let me win the lottery once . . . that's all I'll ever ask for . . . just let me win and I'll never bother you again!" Over and over for several years he uttered the same prayer. Then one night, he had a dream that

God appeared to him and spoke these words: "You've got to meet me halfway. At least buy a ticket!"

In 1943, a young family was vacationing together when the father asked his three-year-old daughter to pose for a picture. As soon as he took the photo she demanded to see it, but he explained that she had to wait until they went home so he could have the film developed into a print. This excuse didn't satisfy the child. She still wanted to open the camera and see the picture he had taken.

Suddenly the father remembered one of his favorite sayings: "Creativity is the sudden cessation of stupidity." In that instant, he realized that his three-year-old probably reflected the frustrations of millions of other people. When they take a picture, they want to see right then how it came out. So, accepting his daughter's challenge, he set a goal for himself to create equipment that would allow for instantaneous development of film.

Most of us don't have the ability to reach that goal and it would be unrealistic for us to set it. However, Edwin Land, the father in this story, had the knowledge and ability and he was determined to make it happen. When he was seventeen he dropped out of Harvard University to work on a product that he felt would save lives by eliminating the glare of automobile headlights. He developed a patent for polarized lenses, which he later applied to sunglasses.

Now, thanks to his daughter's impatience, he had another goal. Eventually he came up with more than one hundred original, patented inventions before the process worked as he had envisioned. By the time his daughter was seven, he was able to provide a camera to millions who wanted to see the photo immediately after taking it. Edwin Land, with his natural talent for mechanical engineering and applied science, became the father of the self-developing camera and started one of the most successful companies in America. And today, on the campus of

Harvard University, there's a building that looks very much like a gigantic Polaroid camera!

2. Having taken responsibility for your own success, do you still take into account the help you'll need from others?

Everyone needs help from others to succeed. You need ongoing contact with people who have more experience or who have access to resources and contacts that you don't have. I call this gaining all the expertise you can, while always avoiding thinking like an expert.

Observe the leaders in your chosen field. Study how they think about their work and their lives in general. Most important, find out how they solve problems and create opportunities.

You can identify these leaders by reading trade publications and by talking to others in your field. Which names keep appearing? Who is quoted most often? Once you identify these individuals, read what they've written and what has been written about them. Seek them out in person by attending their lectures and seminars. Make personal contact. You might even start a file on each one of them. Ask yourself, what are these leaders doing that sets them apart? Is there anything about their personal or professional style that you can adopt and use?

Peak performers are often more focused on the future, more determined, more tuned in to the places where ideas happen. They pick up ideas and information by being alert and open. When some trend comes along, they pay attention. They write it down in their journal to think about later.

Don't ever wait for your phone calls to be returned, or for your letters to be answered. Don't wait for mentors to seek you out. Richard P. Feynman, the Nobel-prize–winning physicist, advised, ''Seek out people who don't hold you in awe, who are willing to challenge you, even if they're wrong.'' Unless you encourage them to do otherwise, most people will tell you what they think you want to hear. Get feedback about your goals that is honest and objective. Listen attentively when your assumptions are challenged. Refuse to allow yourself to become defensive. This is the kind of relationship we referred to earlier, in connection with the "sounding boards" in the Personal Inventory section of your journal. By the way, Richard Feynman practiced what he preached. His exalted status as a scientist and professor didn't prevent him from taking drawing lessons, dancing lessons, and even bongo-drum lessons.

In bouncing your goals off other people, there are two serious traps to avoid. The first is assuming that you're a novice and that your ideas are not good enough to be field-tested and discussed with experts. The other trap is already considering yourself to be an expert in your field. Sir Clive Sinclair, the British inventor of the pocket calculator and the flat-screen television, among other things, says that when he enters a new field he reads just enough to get a basic understanding and then begins asking questions. Being too much of an expert can actually get in your way. Henry Ford described an expert as an individual who "knew all the reasons an idea wouldn't work."

3. Have you examined your individual goals in terms of importance and difficulty of attainment?

One of the major roadblocks to goal achievement is trying to hit a quick home run instead of winning the game with a series of base hits. Mike Schmidt, the great Philadelphia Phillies third baseman who was inducted into the baseball Hall of Fame in 1995, said, "Whenever I hit a ball out of the park, I had been trying to hit it on the ground." Research has shown that when people go after one big goal in one big step, they invariably fail. If you tried to swallow a twelve-ounce steak with one gulp, you'd choke. You've got to cut it into small pieces and eat one bite at a time.

The vocabulary of most Americans includes between nine hundred and two thousand words. If you could learn just two new words each day, within a year you could be increasing your word power by a significant percentage. While serving time in prison as a young man, Malcolm X decided to rise above his former life as a street thug and become a force for social change. His first step was to procure an edition of Webster's dictionary from the prison library and start copying. In fact, Malcolm X copied the entire dictionary three times. Years later he made a special visit to New York's American Museum of Natural History in order to view the stuffed aardvark on display there. After all, the aardvark was not only one of the strangest-sounding animals he'd ever read about—it was also the first word in the dictionary!

Once you start thinking incrementally in terms of achieving your goals, you'll realize how much you can really accomplish. Read three pages of a book each day . . . write two letters . . . meet one new person—by taking things one step at a time, you can literally transform your life.

Make sure that the sizable goals you've set for yourself include all the steps necessary to achieve them. Then start taking those steps one at a time. That's the secret to turning those mini-goals into maximum accomplishment.

4. Do any of your goals require you to act in a way that's completely out of step with your temperament and character?

Are your goals really consistent with the person you want to be? A friend of mine, a writer, was asked a number of years ago to help out with the political campaign of a person running for a local office. She accepted the position at 6:00 P.M., but after thinking about it overnight, she phoned the next day at 8:00 A.M. to resign.

"What prompted your decision?" I asked her.

She said, "I thought long and hard about what it would mean to be a political writer—concerned with slogans, speeches, and soundbites. On the one hand, it was a new challenge. On the other, I couldn't think of anything I'd enjoy doing less.''

The candidate won the election and eventually went on to become governor of the state in which my friend lives. I pointed out to her one day that she might well have been the press spokesperson for the governor's office had she pursued that initial campaign position. She replied, ''Yes, and I think I could have done the quality of work that would have made me an asset for just that type of position. I also think I would have been miserable had I done that. I would have missed other opportunities that have brought me great joy and satisfaction. Accomplishment in the eyes of others? Yes. A feeling of personal success? No.''

Don't play to any audience other than the one you see in the mirror. Do what is consistent with your values, your beliefs, your understanding of your personality, and of what brings you fulfillment.

Don't set unrealistic goals for yourself in areas where you have limited abilities or experience. If you have questions about your natural talents, I suggest that you consider taking an aptitude test of the type offered by the nonprofit Johnson O'Connor Research Foundation in New York City, which has testing facilities in major cities throughout the United States.

5. Is the time frame you envision for goal achievement both challenging and realistic?

It's important to make a distinction between the time you allot for achieving your major, life-forming goals, and the schedules you set for your subgoals, or short-term objectives.

For subgoals, you should have a time frame challenging enough so that your deadlines take some real effort to meet, but realistic enough so that you reach your objectives on schedule at least half the time. If you're always reaching your time-specific goals easily, you may want to demand more from yourself. But if your subgoals are always taking more time than you expected, break them down into still smaller bites so that you get the positive reinforcement of achievement on a regular basis.

On the other hand, I believe you should be extremely flexible about setting time limits for your life-forming goals, and you probably should not set any at all. During World War II, the Russian and Nazi armies were engaged in a prolonged life-or-death struggle on the eastern front. An American officer was sent by President Roosevelt to meet with the commander of the Russian forces, General Georgi Zhukov. The American asked how long Zhukov expected the Russians' battle against the Nazis to continue, and what would be the price in lives and equipment. The grizzled Russian officer replied that he never asked himself how long the war would take or what it would cost, because he believed that setting a mental limit on such an enormous undertaking would somehow cause the actual toll to be higher. "However many months or years I predict it will take," Zhukov said, "it will surely take longer. And however many men I say will die, there will surely be more."

Seeing his visitor's disappointment with this answer, General Zhukov added, "I'm sorry I can't be more specific in my answers to your questions. But there is one thing I can tell you with great certainty."

"What is it?" the American asked.

"That we are going to win."

6. Finally, have you considered the obstacles that you may encounter, and have you devised ways to turn them to your advantage?

Dealing with obstacles is so critically important that the entire next chapter is devoted to it. Right now, however, I would like to make one very important point in this regard, and it's one that may surprise you: *Not every obstacle can be overcome!* Not every problem has a solution. Every woman can't act like Meryl Streep, and every man can't dance like Fred Astaire. It just isn't in the cards. But even though this is true, I still believe the best strategy for success includes a firm belief in your ability to control every aspect of your own destiny. Try to make a realistic assessment of your abilities and the difficulties you'll have to overcome in order to achieve your goals, but it's far better to overestimate yourself and then try your hardest than it is to simply stay where you are because the climb looks too steep. My experience with thousands of achievers in all walks of life has shown me that very few people are grossly off the mark in evaluating their own ability and potential. Most men really know they can't sing like Pavarotti—I certainly know it!

Keeping Track of Progress

Once you've evaluated your goals in terms of these six categories, don't just set them aside. Use your journal to assess your progress. A good way to do this is by writing a nightly progress report: Take ten minutes every evening to describe the things you did that day that will help you reach your goals. Make note of situations that you might want to handle differently in the future, record obstacles, and chart the positive experiences you'll want to repeat. If you find that you didn't accomplish everything you'd intended to, give the things left undone top priority for the following day. These progress reports will provide you with a broader perspective on what you're doing right and what you could be doing better.

One of my mentors, the late Earl Nightingale, told me a story about a farmer walking through a field planted with a crop of pumpkins. The farmer came across a glass jug that apparently had been thrown in his field by a passing motorist. As an experiment, he poked a very small, green pumpkin through the neck of the bottle.

Months later, when the field was fully developed and about ready for harvesting, the farmer again came across the glass jug. The other pumpkins on the same vine were large and fully developed, but the pumpkin in the jug had not been able to grow beyond the confines of the glass, and was shaped to its exact dimensions. What kind of jug are *you* struggling to grow in? When you enlarge the size and scope of your goals, and when you create a detailed blueprint for achievement, your dreams can take any shape you care to give them. In other words, your success can be as big as you dare to envision it.

CHAPTER SEVEN

Flextactic: Turn Obstacles into Opportunities

Even for "Overnight Successes," the Night Can Be Rather Long

The achievements that we cherish most are those we have worked hardest to gain. The farther we've come, the sweeter the celebration at the destination when we arrive. These are simply facts of human psychology, and it's important to keep them in mind when obstacles appear on the path to your goals. No matter how forbidding or potentially destructive these obstacles seem, in the long run they'll make your achievements even more satisfying.

Too often we assume that successful people just happened to get a string of lucky breaks. In reality, the opposite is usually true: Many a superstar had an incredibly rough time before he or she attained any lasting success. There was, for instance, a laundry worker who earned sixty dollars a week but had a burning desire to be a writer. He spent his nights and weekends typing manuscripts to send to publishers and agents. Each one was rejected with a form letter that gave him no assurance that his manuscript had even been read. Finally, a more encouraging rejection letter arrived. It said that although the laundry worker's writing was not yet publishable, he should keep trying. So over the next eighteen months he sent two more manuscripts, but these were rejected as well. Finances got so tight for this young man and his wife that they had to disconnect their telephone to pay for medicine for their baby. Feeling totally discouraged, he threw his latest work into the garbage. But his wife, totally committed to his life goals and believing in his talent, rescued the manuscript from the trash and submitted it to the publisher. The book, titled *Carrie,* sold over five million copies. The laundry worker, of course, was Stephen King.

One well-known woman broadcaster was fired eighteen times, which might make the *Guinness Book of World Records*! But every time she got fired, she went after something bigger and better, using her obstacles as stepping-stones toward more responsible positions. When no mainland radio station would hire her, she learned Spanish and moved to Puerto Rico. When a wire service refused to send her to cover a revolution in a Latin American country, she flew there at her own expense to write and sell freelance stories. Finally, years later, she went on the air talking about issues that were important to her and inviting callers to express their personal opinions. Today, Sally Jessy Rafael has won several Emmy awards, and has her own TV show reaching 8 million viewers a day. She says, "I could have let those eighteen firings prevent me from doing what I wanted. Instead, I used them to spur me on."

At the age of sixty Thomas Edison wrote, "I'll never give up, because I may have a streak of luck before I die. From now until I'm 75, I expect to be busy with my regular work. At 75, I expect to wear loud waistcoats with fancy buttons. At 80, I expect to learn to play bridge and talk foolish to the ladies, and at 85 to wear a full dress suit every evening at dinner. At 90— well, I never plan more than 30 years ahead."

Turning Stumbling Blocks into Stepping-stones

When I asked you to list your strengths, talents, and abilities in your journal, there may have been qualities that you would have liked to include but were unable to do so honestly. Now it's time to face up to the areas of weakness in your life and seek to make them strong.

Weaknesses should always be evaluated in light of your life-forming goals. You may not be able to run with a football like the Detroit Lions' Barry Sanders, but do your goals really require you to run with a football at all? On the other hand, you *must* be able to face up to the areas of deficiency that are in fact related to your objectives. As long as those areas remain, they will block your road to maximum success. Chaos, you'll recall, includes a "sensitive dependence on initial conditions." You need to know at the outset where the ripples may turn into waves.

Right now, take a moment to identify five things about yourself that you believe you need to strengthen to reach your goals in the allotted time. Identify these areas of weakness, and add them in your journal as your Personal Inventory Postscript. Promise yourself that you will begin actively seeking growth, development, or change in these areas, so that they will not be a part of your permanent personal inventory. They should be temporary items that you are hoping to eliminate as negatives and add as positives within weeks or months.

Also in your Personal Inventory Postscript, include matters of health and physical fitness, education and experience, character and personality. Along with each area of weakness, describe the means by which you intend to turn it into a strength. Don't expect to convert all of your weaknesses into strengths before you begin to implement your goals. After all, nothing will ever be attempted in life if all objections must first be overcome.

Don't wait. But do expect to work on your weaknesses as you pursue success. Make their remedy a goal in and of itself.

After identifying your areas of weakness, write down what I call an Obstacle Checklist. What major problems or deficiencies are keeping you from success? In my seminars, I offer the following list as an example:

- negative childhood environment
- inadequate education
- too many dependents and responsibilities
- bad economic conditions or government policies
- insufficient capital or bad credit
- uncooperative spouse
- discrimination
- chemical dependency
- obsolete industry
- born in the wrong place or time

Now understand this truth: *Nearly every well-known achiever in history before you has faced those same obstacles, and many more.*

Negative childhood environment? Colin Powell, former chairman of the Joint Chiefs of Staff, grew up in the tough South Bronx section of New York City and mopped floors to help support his family. Powell wasn't humiliated by his floor-mopping experience. On the contrary, he's proud of the fact that he became an outstanding mopper, and he's written that he could still get out there and mop as well as anyone.[6]

Inadequate education? Well, learning isn't confined to schools, and knowledge is always available to those who are determined to acquire it. As I write this, Bill Gates of Microsoft is the wealthiest person in America, yet Gates is a college dropout who largely taught himself everything he needed to know about software, beginning with his membership in a computer club when he was in the eighth grade.

Although Bill Gates came from a relatively comfortable background, other highly successful individuals have overcome severe disadvantages. In fact, the most inspiring turnaround I know of is the story of my friend Joe Sorrentino, the son of a Brooklyn sanitation worker, who believed he was "born to lose."

An incorrigible juvenile delinquent, Joe was always fighting and causing trouble in his neighborhood, and was finally expelled from high school in his freshman year. After a brief enlistment in the Marine Corps, he was dishonorably discharged. But then, in a moment of truth, he took control of his life. Returning to night school at the age of twenty, Joe Sorrentino graduated with honors from the University of California. Then, to clear his bad military record, he reenlisted in the Marine Corps and became the first person in history to receive an honorable discharge after having been previously discharged under less than honorable conditions. He became a student leader at Harvard Law School and an outstanding juvenile court judge in Los Angeles. When I last saw him, he had written a number of best-selling books and was a law professor and one of the most sought-after platform speakers in America.

The obstacles that you see blocking your way are really, for the most part, your own learned perceptions. They are misinformed prejudices against yourself, and prejudice limits vision. Prejudice keeps you focused on what you *think* exists, rather than what *can and should* exist. Prejudice stifles creativity and prevents problem solving. It insists that there is only one way of looking at a situation, because "that's just the way things are."

Five years ago there were a lot of people willing to pay for a quick cup of good coffee, but in most places there wasn't much they could do about it. There simply weren't many outlets for high-quality coffee on the run. But few people considered this a real problem, let alone a chance to start a successful business. They just thought, "I'd like a cup of good coffee, but there's no convenient place to get one. That's just the way things are." Well, today all those people are forming lines in the hundreds of Starbucks coffee shops that have sprung up all over the country, because there *was* an opportunity to change things, and it was just waiting for somebody to take advantage of it.

Here are some additional Flex-Planning ideas:

Schedule longer, uninterrupted blocks of time for special projects.
Most important inventions, breakthrough innovations, and great works of art are created during uninterrupted time frames. In my own experience, each book or program I have written has been done by working twelve to seventeen hours a day for a specific number of days. Granted, I may have sacrificed a ski trip or a week or two at the beach. But because I focused on prime projects in prime time, the return on invested resources has been richly rewarding.

Prepare for delays and plan for interruptions.
Mark time on your calendar to account for them. One of my weaknesses is becoming overcommitted as a result of not properly anticipating constant interruptions in my schedule. You should always have a Plan B when your Plan A hits a snag—a traffic jam, a canceled flight, or someone showing up late for a meeting. Ask yourself, "How can I use ten minutes here and five minutes there to help me reach my goals?" My wife, Susan, carries a small piece of needlework with her at all times. She uses the "spare moments" of her life to make seasonal and special gifts, virtually all of which are completed with a few stitches now, a few stitches later.

Ask yourself, "If I knew I had exactly twenty years left to live, what would I do differently in terms of goal setting and priorities?"

Then ask yourself what you would do differently if you had only *one* year left. How can you mesh those two answers into a plan? Remember, a goal is not really a goal until all the substeps are mapped out in time. Unless a plan is translated into hours, days, and deadlines, there's little likelihood you will enact it. You'll spin your wheels in frustration, procrastinate, or rush into action without direction. I once overheard a flight instructor say to a cadet, "Where are we in relation to the target?" The cadet responded, "I'm not sure, but we're making great speed, sir!" Forward motion without direction leads to failure. Forward motion with direction, and sequenced in time, leads to success.

But even with all the steps mapped out, you must be able to readjust your goals.

What would happen if the steps you needed to reach your goals didn't turn out the way you planned? To prepare for this possibility, ask yourself how changing one subgoal would affect all your other objectives. Let yourself see how one step has the possibility to affect every other step along the way.

If your first plan fails . . . regroup and try again!

Plans are not set in concrete. They are put on paper, and are generally best written with pencils that have erasers. Many a championship has been won after the first round was lost. Each setback should be just one more source of information to consider as you create a new and better plan.

Sometimes fortunes are made from solutions to problems that do not necessarily arise in direct relation to a stated goal.

Josephine Garis Cochrane found that every time she served dinner using her good china, she broke at least one precious piece when she washed the dishes. So she set up a shop in the woodshed behind her house, twisted wire in the shape of a rack and attached it to a wire wheel, stuck it in a box, and mounted it on top of a copper tank full of hot, soapy water. She attached a hand crank and spun the dish rack around while the hot water showered her cups and saucers. The crude device worked, and her friends were so impressed that they urged her to patent and manufacture it. Today, Josephine Cochrane's KitchenAid automatic dishwasher is still the standard of the industry.

Never forget that today's obstacles can become tomorrow's corporations.
A person with a flexible, inventive mind will find a new product where someone else sees only an annoying deprivation. That kind of problem offers for free something that entrepreneurs work hard and spend a great deal of money to create—a demand or a market. The more frustrating and widespread the difficulty, the greater the demand for a product or service that can end the frustration. It's all just a matter of seeing something that others miss.

With the exception of the personal computer, I believe that no innovation in the past twenty-five years has had a greater impact on American life than the introduction of the running shoe. In the days when the only available athletic shoes were the old-fashioned canvas sneakers, long-distance running was virtually impossible for the general public. Yet a great deal of attention was already being paid to the need for improved fitness, and there was a vast demand waiting to be filled. When running shoes became available, shoe styles—and lifestyles—very quickly changed for millions of people. In fact, the whole economy of the world was altered, as the new shoes by the millions began to be manufactured overseas. Today, I doubt there is a single household in America without several pairs of running shoes in the closet—and I'm sure it will soon be possible to make the same statement about China, with its more than a billion pairs of feet!

CHAPTER EIGHT

Flextactic: Be Selective to Gain the Most from Today

The Choice Is Yours

Earlier, we discussed the First Law of Thermodynamics, which states that the energy put into any closed system will always be balanced by the energy going out. Transposed into human terms, this simply means that the quality and quantity of your efforts will determine the results you obtain.

This is hardly a new insight, though it's certainly a very important one. "As you sow, so shall you reap" is how the Bible expresses it. An acronym from the computer industry—GIGO, or "garbage in, garbage out"—puts the same idea even more succinctly.

This is one of the eternal, fundamental laws that govern each of our lives. If we make good use of our minds, our skills, and our talents, there will be rewards in all areas of our lives. If we take personal responsibility for making the best possible use of all our resources in the time we have, there will be enormous gains in personal happiness, success, and wealth. This is true of everyone's life—yet scarcely one in a thousand individuals ever puts his or her time to anywhere near its optimum use. We tend to *let* things happen *to* us, when we should be *making* things happen *for* us.

One of the greatest blessings of our free society is the sheer number of choices and opportunities we have. When I interviewed our returning POWs from Vietnam, as well as the former hostages from the takeover of the American Embassy in Iran, both groups indicated that what they missed most during their captivity was their "freedom of choice." In my opinion, among all the many choices we are free to make, one in particular is of paramount importance. It is the choice between simply accepting things as they are, or accepting the responsibility for changing them for the better.

A recent University of California at Berkeley study indicates that personal happiness is directly related to having a sense of control over one's life. When that sense of control is present, people seem to choose more effective responses to whatever takes place. They're able to face unexpected changes, and even chaos, with less apprehension. Rather than endlessly replaying mistakes, they learn from them. They spend time "doing" in the present, rather than "stewing" about the past or the future and fearing what may happen next. They are proactive, not reactive.

There is also, of course, an opposite type of individual— one who believes in luck, fate, astrological predetermination, and "you can't fight city hall." These people are likely to procrastinate, to give in to fears and doubts, and to suffer emotional and physical problems as a result. They see themselves as victims of the system. But when we become aware of the thousands of individuals who have overcome every possible hardship to achieve greatness, we realize that in this abundant nation, many victims of the system are actually volunteers who are collaborating in their own failure.

Using Time Efficiently

In a 1993 *New York Times* interview, Peter Middleton, the new CEO of Lloyd's of London, talked about the huge losses recently suffered by the prestigious insurance company after three hundred years of sterling performance. Middleton said, "Lloyd's got very complacent in the mid-1980s and believed that its tomorrows would always be as good as its todays. That's fatal thinking in any business, and especially in insurance, with its built-in uncertainties."

Peter Middleton believes that Lloyd's was afflicted by "the British disease where people are wholly task-oriented, and where success means moving a pile of paper from an 'In' tray to an 'Out' tray. These people feel uncomfortable sitting at their desks thinking about what they should really be doing next. But they should be thinking about that for a significant part of the day. Otherwise, how do you know you're giving the right direction and emphasis to whatever you actually do?"

Middleton is addressing a very important problem: How can we recognize the best ways to use our time? How can we think productively so that we can work productively?

One of the human mind's most fascinating qualities is its ability to program itself. When you really need to awaken at a certain hour, for example, you can "set the alarm" in your mind, and you'll usually wake up at the right time. Similarly, most people have an intuitive sense of what time it is, even if they work indoors and don't have access to a clock. And many people have conditioned themselves over the years to do certain things at certain times almost automatically, such as taking medication or checking on small children.

This inherent ability can help make you aware of your most productive periods of the day. It's simply a matter of listening to your body and of discovering what works best for you. For many people, the early morning is a time of maximum productivity. If that's true of you, set aside the morning for your most important work. Don't clutter up your most important hours with routine activities and busywork.

Other people really begin to come alive in the afternoon. They drag through the morning hours until a burst of energy finally kicks them into high gear. If that sounds like you, reserve the afternoon hours for your most important priorities.

I've been fortunate enough to have seen a large number of world-class athletes in action. There's an amazing efficiency of motion about these people; they don't even seem to be working. In reaching your goals, strive to produce a quality result without wasted effort and with a minimum of time invested.

Let me say it as efficiently as possible: Don't work harder, work smarter!

"What Happens If I Don't Do This?"

Recently I gave a seminar at ADIA Personnel Services, a successful human resources firm, where I happened to see a survey of more than a thousand executives who were asked what it takes to become a top-notch manager. Fifty-eight percent said that strong personal qualities, including integrity and self-reliance, were crucial to getting ahead. Being results-oriented came in a close second (54 percent), as did being ambitious (47 percent). The ability to recognize and take advantage of an opportunity was considered important by 24 percent of those polled. But only 9 percent of the executives felt that taking on extra work was a significant ingredient.

The key is not to put in more effort but to give all of your attention to the right task at the right moment; to work *with* time, rather than against it; to focus your energies on important projects during the hours in which you are biologically and psychologically "up"; and to eliminate time-wasting activities from your schedule.

Be aware that many time-wasting activities disguise themselves as important business. Before you begin any task, ask yourself a few simple, straightforward questions: Is this real work or fake work? What happens if I don't do this? Will anything be different for better or worse? What will be the consequences if I don't put this in writing? What will be the likely outcome of this memo? Will a two-minute conversation be just as effective?

A survey conducted by consultants at Robert Half International concluded that top executives spend 22 percent of their time—as much as eleven work weeks per year—writing or reading memos. The one hundred executives polled added that they considered almost half of those memos to be a waste of time. If that's true, a great many managers are spending one month a year writing memos that don't need to be written!

I'm always amazed by people who fill their weekly and monthly calendars with dozens of activities—scheduling all of their time to go places and do things—and they call this goal setting. Yet the only goal they achieve is being overtired, overextended and overobligated.

Don't assume that the more you schedule, the more you really get done. You can go to a group meeting or seminar every night for the next year and be no closer to your goals. Chinese philosopher Lin Yutang said it simply: "Besides the noble art of getting things done, there is the noble art of leaving things undone. The wisdom of life consists in the elimination of nonessentials."

Much of the activity in our lives is really habit. We do countless things every day without thinking about them—from the way we brush our teeth to the order in which we put on our shoes and socks. Part of planning for success is breaking old habits and beginning to bring a new flexibility into your life.

Begin each day with this question: "What am I going to do today that will be the best use of my time and energy and that will bring me a step closer to achieving my goals?" During the day, each time you are faced with a decision, ask yourself, "Does this action substantially help me toward achieving my goals?" With practice, this way of thinking will become instinctive, and once it does, you'll be amazed at how many things are always trying to crop up between you and your objectives. Telephone calls are among the most common time wasters. Coworkers who stop by to chat are another . . . messy files that slow down your ability to find important items . . . disorganized scheduling . . . a cluttered desk. Take an objective look at your working environment, and then take action!

You may want to hold your calls for a period of time so you can concentrate on creative projects. Then you can return your calls at a convenient time each day. You may need to close your office door for an hour or two, even though you normally have an open-door policy. You may even need to spend a day or two simply getting organized, cleaning out your office, or combining your appointment calendars into one master schedule. I call this "cleaning out the closets of my mind," and I do it once a month.

Before leaving your workplace at the end of the day, make a list of your priorities for the following day in the order of their importance. I divide my activities into A, B, and C lists: A is for action immediately, B is before the end of the day, and C can be put off until later. If you find that you're giving top priority to too many items, you're probably not breaking your goals down far enough. Instead of keeping them separate and manageable, you may be combining too many elements into one task.

One of the most effective time-management consultants in

the nation, in my opinion, is my colleague Lyle Sussman, professor of management at the University of Louisville. His action steps for maximizing productivity have helped thousands of executives, myself included. I have added to and improvised a sample checkoff list drawn from his outstanding guidebook, *Smart Moves,* co-written by Sam Deep and Lyle Sussman and published by Addison-Wesley.[7] I call this list Twenty-one Ways to Make Time Your Slave:

1. Record in one calendar-planning system like Franklin, Day-Timer, or Day-Runner all the projects and people you manage. Write down in the action section every commitment you make at the time you make it, and then transfer that commitment to the date in the calendar when it will come due. Put your daily "to do" list on the first page in that planner, and change it every day.

2. Plan each week the week before, and plan each day the day before. Spend forty minutes at the beginning of each week, and fifteen to twenty minutes the night before or at the beginning of each day planning your "to do" list. Ask yourself, "What will I accomplish this week and this new day?"

3. Stop wasting the first hour of your workday. Having that extra cup of coffee, reading the newspaper, and socializing are the three opening rituals that cost the most in lower productivity.

4. Do one thing at a time, and do it well. It takes time to start and stop work on each activity. Stay with a project until it is completed.

5. Create a time-analysis chart of your activities. Break your day into fifteen-minute blocks. Note your chief activity or activities for each block. After logging your activities for a week or so, you'll have a representative

sample of how your time is spent. Study the results. Decide what you can do to make better use of your time.

6. Establish time limits for meetings and conversations in advance. Consult your watch when a deadline approaches. End the conversation when it arrives. Wristwatch alarms or beepers can be effective tools in keeping meetings within limits.

7. Don't open unimportant junk mail. At least 25 percent of the mail you receive can be thrown away without taking the time to open it.

8. Try to handle each piece of paper only once—including faxes, letters, and memos—and never more than twice. Don't set anything aside without taking some action. Some executives carry briefcases full of faxes, letters, and memos around for days without taking action. By the time they act, they are often too late to capitalize on the opportunity. For you as a twenty-first century achiever, one computer disk for a notebook computer is better than a steamer trunk full of papers.

9. Carry work, reading material, audiotapes, and your laptop computer with you everywhere you go. Convert downtime into uplink time.

10. Write answers in the margins of letters you receive and mail or fax the letter back to the sender.

11. Recognize when your peak energy occurs during the day. Allocate the most difficult projects to that period. Work on easy projects at low-energy times.

12. When you feel that your energy level is dropping, take a break. For many people, this occurs around three in the afternoon. For you, it may be in the early morning or right after lunch.

13. Get enough rest, nutrients, and exercise. If you don't feel well, you can't do well. Maintain your health and

build your stamina. Treat your body the way you would if it were a space shuttle you were about to be launched in. Treat yourself as if you are worth the effort and expense it takes to nurture yourself!

14. Set aside personal relaxation time during the day. Don't work during lunch. It's neither noble nor nutritional to skip important energy-input and stress-relieving times.

15. Take shorter vacations more often and leave your work at home. The harder you work, the more you need to balance your exercise and your leisure time.

16. When possible, plan your work so your projects end when your day does. Take work home only as an exception, not the rule. Your professional life needs a whole human being, one with a satisfying personal life.

17. End the day by listing all of tomorrow's important priorities. Incorporate these projects into your daily "to do" list.

18. Throughout the day, ask yourself, "What's the best use of my time right now?" As the day grows short, focus on projects you can least afford to leave undone.

19. Each day, take some time to focus on your long-term dreams. You will keep your motivation vivid and strong. I take a walk of at least fifteen minutes every day, rain, snow, or shine. If the weather is bad, I walk through an indoor mall. While I am walking and exercising, I think about my life goals. It's a great way to window-shop, and if I keep walking it saves money too!

20. (You may not get too excited about this suggestion, but it has worked wonders for me.) Consider getting up forty minutes earlier in the morning and going to bed forty minutes earlier. You may need to inch into this habit by setting your alarm ten minutes earlier each week for four weeks. The extra forty minutes in the

morning can become some of your most productive, personally rewarding "home alone" time. Use the forty minutes to think about what is really important for you to accomplish with this full day ahead of you. By going to bed forty minutes earlier, you may have to sacrifice a few one-liners by Jay Leno or David Letterman, but they won't mind, and after all, they are well on their way to reaching their life goals, while not the least bit concerned with you reaching yours.

21. Make certain your television set is in a cabinet that has a door on it that you can close. Treat it as it deserves to be treated. It is just one of your appliances, not your trusted armchair or bedside companion. The average American adult spends about thirty hours per week in a TV-induced stupor. Children spend even more time this way, which is why they are out of shape and also why they are staying home longer after they graduate from high school and college. They are used to tension-relieving activities, rather than goal-achieving actions.

What You're Really Killing When You're "Just Killing Time"

When you kill time, you kill your opportunities for success. Imagine what could really be accomplished in the thirty hours a week that most people spend watching television! Thirty hours a week amounts to nearly sixteen hundred hours a year. How many books or articles could you read in that time? How many new people could you meet and learn from?

Time is our most precious possession. It's far more valuable than money. I know many multimillionaires who would gladly give a million dollars just to live another year or two in good

91

health. The successful person knows how to put energy into time and draw success from time.

Time has a dual structure. First, we must live out our daily routines, dealing with contingencies as they arise. Second, our most ambitious goals and desires need time to be assembled and secured. A long-term goal connects pieces of time into one block. These blocks can be imagined and projected into the future as goals that we set for ourselves, or they can be created in retrospect as we look back at what we've accomplished.

My friend Bob Smullin, who founded the Day Focus System, says he has never met an individual with clearly focused objectives who also has a time-management problem. On the other hand, Bob says he knows many people who have time-management problems because they lack well-defined objectives.

Loss of focus and motivation isn't caused by having dreams that are too big. On the contrary, it's the drudgery and routine of our daily lives that present the greatest danger to achieving our objectives. Imagine your life-forming goals as large, friendly dogs, and your daily "to do" lists as a collection of little fleas. Get rid of some fleas every day, and the dogs will become what they were meant to be: man's best friends!

CHAPTER NINE

Flextactic: Think Positively About Your Work

Beauty Is in the Eye of the Beholder, and So Is Hard Work

Any challenge in life should be faced with enthusiasm and a good sense of humor, but if we think of challenges as chores, sooner or later we're going to simply give up. In order to stay motivated and focused for the hard work required to reach your goals, try to view that work with the same excitement and anticipation as you would recreation or an adventurous vacation.

That's not really as difficult as it sounds. Our experience of work is largely determined by our own perceptions and expectations. After being at sea all week, a professional fisherman may want to relax by doing some gardening on Saturday and Sunday. Conversely, a professional gardener might want to go fishing to get away from his work. I like the story of the airline pilot who, on another routine cross-country flight, was looking out the cockpit window at the beautiful Minnesota lakes far below, wishing he could retire and just sit in a rowboat. At the same moment, a boy in a rowboat was looking up in awe at the vapor trails of the passing jetliner, wishing he could fly that plane!

I was a close friend of the late Dr. Hans Selye, who did pioneering research in the field of stress. Dr. Selye liked to say that he had never worked a day in his life, although he was up at 5:00 A.M. and stayed in his laboratory until late at night. He said he was "playing" all that time, because to Dr. Selye research was play. Every achiever I know loves his or her work and is oblivious to the passage of time due to the total involvement in that work. That's why I believe that to be a successful goal setter, you must find ways to think positively about your work.

The Glass is Half Full!

The importance of a positive attitude toward work holds true for young people as well as for seasoned veterans of the corporate wars. I know a student who received such a high score on her Law School Admissions Test that she was hired to teach a class on how to succeed on the exam. She told her students that the key to doing well was the ability to view the test as a unique experience and an interesting challenge.

In a study comparing one thousand randomly selected American children to an equal number of Asian boys and girls, researchers at the University of Michigan isolated no differences in general aptitudes and abilities. They did find, however, that Chinese and Japanese children attended school 240 days a year, compared to only 178 days for American kids. A century and a half ago, American children were given two and a half months away from school so that they could help their parents harvest crops; now the two and a half months are spent at the mall or the beach.

A second major area of difference revealed in these studies concerns basic perceptions of education. While fifth graders in Minneapolis spend about 46 minutes a day on homework (well above the national average, by the way), Chinese children spend about 114 minutes—but they don't call it homework, they call it home education. Asian children enjoy doing their home education projects and aren't ashamed to admit it. Most American children hate their homework and seem proud to say so. This isn't really surprising, either, since American mothers and fathers tell their kids, "As soon as you get your work done, you can have fun and watch TV."

We tend to believe that children succeed in school according to innate talents and abilities. Japanese and Chinese parents are more likely to say that their children succeed or fail based on the quality of their effort. And the productivity results from the Asian countries indicate that these efforts are paying off. Some futurists are even referring to the twenty-first century as the Pacific Rim Century, because of the shifting of the balance of global economic power toward that region.

The attitudes toward work that we develop in childhood are likely to persist throughout our lives. Too many of us regard our jobs as dull and repetitive, an irritating interruption between weekends. I recently heard someone say, "The only joy I get at work is when the little hand reaches five." This is a feeling shared by countless people, many of whom do have less than stimulating jobs. But the statement I quoted was made by a high-ranking corporate executive. His salary is in the high six figures, he keeps two assistants busy, and he oversees the work of five hundred employees from behind his big mahogany desk. You may envy his position. You may think, "Nice work, if you can get it." Yet this executive finds his work taxing, stressful, and tedious. Whatever enthusiasm he may have used in order to attain his position has sadly been lost along the way.

Seven Principles That Make Hard Work Hard but Enjoyable

I believe that joy of achievement occurs in direct proportion to the effort expended, and that the greatest happiness comes from the realization that we have accomplished something. Personal satisfaction is the most important ingredient of success, though this is something that each person must define for himself or herself.

For a retailer satisfaction might take the form of a satisfied customer, for a financial officer it might be balancing the company's budget, for an artist it might be painting a picture. None of this is simply a matter of dollars and cents. Rather, it's a subjective experience of having fulfilled one's responsibilities despite whatever difficulties and setbacks may have intervened.

Success is never a constant. We believe success, once earned, should be permanent, but genuine success must be constantly renewed. It is not in the pursuit of happiness that we find fulfillment, it is in the happiness of pursuit!

Here are seven ways to make the hard work of pursuing your goals more satisfying and enjoyable:

1. Think of your work as a challenge, not a chore.

If it's something you already know how to do well, try to create new ways for completing the task better or faster. In his book *Excellence,* which is one of my favorites, John W. Gardner emphasizes the principle that doing something really well, however humble the task may seem, is of much greater value than undertaking a grandiose enterprise and doing a mediocre job of it. As Gardner puts it, "an excellent plumber is infinitely more admirable than an incompetent philosopher." Or, as they say in show business, "There are no small parts, only small actors."

My friend Lisa is an example of a great talent with a small

part. She came to New York City fresh out of college, looking for a job in publishing. No one was hiring. Finally, economic necessity made her take a job as a waitress in a coffee shop, where, undaunted, she did her best. She did her work professionally and always greeted each person with courtesy and a smile. One day a regular customer said to her, "I'll bet you aren't a waitress all the time. What else do you do?"

"Well," she replied, "I'd like to become an editor. So I'm working evenings here and going out on job interviews during the day." As it turned out, the customer was a prominent literary agent who needed a bright assistant. An interview was arranged and she got the job. Lisa put into practice the principle of "doing your best" and bringing something fresh to whatever you do every day.

2. Approach whatever you're doing as if it were your first time.

When faced with routine tasks like typing letters, filling out forms, or chairing a meeting, challenge yourself to approach them from a new angle. Each letter, each form, each meeting is, after all, different. So rather than see all the assignments as a huge mass of work, handle each segment from a fresh perspective. This is especially important in sales presentation. Even if you've recited the benefits of your product or service hundreds of times, it is the first time for the customer in front of you. Make it fresh and interesting, as if it were the first time for you too.

I've been giving keynote speeches four days a week for over fifteen years in cities all over the world. The only way I can maintain my enthusiasm and motivation is to tell myself as I walk out on the stage: "This is brand-new for them, and *you're* brand-new for them, so keep it crisp and upbeat, whatever you do, Denis." It works for me, and I sure hope it works as well for my audiences!

3. Follow the "as if" principle.

When you must do work that is dull and repetitious, do it as if it were interesting. Make a game of your work: Try to surpass a self-imposed quota, discover what personal creativity you can add to the job at hand, attempt to do each portion of the task perfectly. Do your work as if you really enjoy it, as if it were really interesting. An immediate benefit is the ease and rapidity with which you'll accomplish your work. Plus, you'll have a lot more energy at the end of the day.

I have a friend who worked for a while in a fruit-processing plant, pouring baskets of sliced apples from a conveyor belt into a huge vat where they were suffused with salt water. When this was done, he returned the salted apples to the conveyor and began refilling new baskets. For the first few days he was exhausted, then bored, then bored *and* exhausted. In desperation, he came up with the idea of turning the whole process into a game: How many complete cycles of apple-salting could he complete in an hour? How many in a morning? How many in a whole day? Before long he was approaching each of his shifts at the fruit-processing plant as if it were a Super Bowl game. The only problem with his system was the complaints from other workers farther down the line who were being deluged with sliced apples!

4. Keep track of your progress toward your goals and take pride in your accomplishments.

The satisfaction of doing your job well and efficiently, of always moving toward your objective, goes a long way toward making hard work enjoyable. Remember when we were children, and our parents taped our drawings or stories on the refrigerator door? Those reminders of our accomplishments did a lot to build self-esteem and keep motivation high. As adults, our small accomplishments are rarely noticed or featured by others, which is why it's so important to note your own accomplishments as you achieve them.

Take the time to say to yourself, "I'm on the right road. I'm doing OK. I'm succeeding." Too frequently, we become preoccupied with pointing out our flaws and identifying our failures. Become equally adept at citing your achievements. Identify things you are doing now that you weren't doing one month ago, six months ago, a year ago, five years ago. What habits have changed? What progress has been made? Write all these things down in your journal. Doing well once or twice is relatively easy. Continuing to move upward is tough, in part because we so easily revert to old habits and former lifestyles. To succeed in the long run, you need to give yourself regular feedback and positive reinforcement.

Dante Gabriel Rossetti, the famous nineteenth-century poet and artist, was once approached by an elderly man. The old fellow had some sketches and drawings by a young artist he wanted Rossetti to look at—to tell him if they were any good, or if they at least showed potential talent.

Rossetti looked over the batch of sketches and immediately became enthusiastic at the talent they revealed. "Oh, these are good," he said. "This young student has great talent. He should be given every help and encouragement in his career as an artist. He has a great future if he will work hard and stick to it." Rossetti could see that the old fellow was deeply moved. "Who is this fine young artist?" he asked. "Your son or daughter?"

"No," said the old man sadly. "These are my own drawings, done more than forty years ago. If only I had had your praise of my work then! As it is, I gave up too soon."

Don't wait for somebody else to encourage your efforts and to show appreciation for your work. Take pride in your own work on a daily basis.

5. Keep the end result in sight.

Always see the big picture: the ultimate goal you're working for and the benefits that come with it.

During World War II, parachutes were being constructed by the thousands. From the workers' point of view, the job was tedious and repetitive. It involved crouching over a sewing machine eight to ten hours a day, stitching endless lengths of colorless fabric. The result was a formless heap of cloth. But every morning, the workers were told that each stitch was part of a lifesaving operation. As they sewed, they were asked to think that this might be the parachute worn by their husband, their brother, or their son. Although the task was hard and the hours long, the women and men on the assembly line understood their contribution to the larger picture.

The same vision should be applied to each of our goals. The insurance agent who perceives every stack of forms as representing a family with needs, aspirations, and dreams. The autoworker who knows each car is taking someone on a safe and productive journey. The cellular-phone salesman who feels part of a global communication network. The bank executive who understands each customer is working and saving, as she is, toward personal and professional goals. These are the visions that take us through the tedious details and carry us to the top.

6. Set up a dynamic daily routine.

Why are railroads and subways still the most energy-efficient means of transportation? Because they run on a track. Getting into a positive routine or groove—not a rut—will help you become more of a peak performer. The more healthy habits and positive routines that can be worked into your day, the more energy you save that would have been expended on trivial decisions such as what to wear, when and where to eat, and how to use your break time.

I've learned a great deal by studying our Olympic athletes.

I have been observing the athletes preparing for the final Olympiad of the century, in Atlanta, Georgia. They are up and showered by 5:30 A.M. They eat a nutritious breakfast. They reflect on their progress from the day before and study their goals for the day. They do a specific regimen of activities in the morning. They eat a light, nutritious lunch high in complex, fiber-based carbohydrates. They reserve a certain part of the early afternoon for phone calls, media interviews, and study. Then back to their training routine. They take a short, creative break in the afternoon. They continue training until just before suppertime. They have a debriefing session with their coach and trainer in the early evening. They listen to music, relax, and socialize with other champions until bedtime. Prior to going to bed, they plan the next day, call or write a friend or relative; then they get a good night's sleep. They do this six days a week for twelve hundred days, just for the privilege of competing in the Olympics. Competing and *winning* demands even more.

When most people think of a daily routine, they imagine a kind of military regimen. They think a routine means doing the same thing over and over again. But the important thing is not to do the same things every day; it's to create a schedule that minimizes interruptions, trivial activity, and downtime.

Try to *order* your day, not regiment it. Order is not sameness, neatness, or everything in its place. Order is not taking on more than you can manage without having to give up what you really want to do. Order is the opposite of complication. Order is not wasting a lot of time trying to find new things. Order is avoiding a lot of recriminations because you didn't do something you promised. Order is setting an effective agenda with someone else, so neither of you is disappointed. Order is doing in a day what you set out to do. Order frees you. Order lets you get into the swing of a healthy, daily routine and discover how much more control you've gained over your life.

7. Schedule time for relaxation and exercise.

Relaxation and exercise are primary ingredients in creativity and inspiration. Before you can use your imagination effectively, you need to relax your mind and body. Mental relaxation allows the right hemisphere of your brain more freedom because the verbal, judgmental, and analytical left hemisphere is quieted. Physical exercise and relaxation improve circulation, release tension, and put you in touch with your body's strengths and weaknesses.

I was sharing a plane ride with the CEO of a very successful company who has been in the corporate fast lane for over forty years. When he told me he was celebrating his seventieth birthday, I nearly dropped my pretzels into my diet Coke. He was trim, his skin was unwrinkled, he had clear eyes and a completely relaxed manner. Yet when he was thirty-nine, this man had been diagnosed with chronic high blood pressure and hypoglycemia. Every weekday thereafter, he had scheduled one hour at the middle of the day for swimming laps at his local health club. When I inquired about luncheon meetings, he said his policy was to have after-lunch meetings. "All people do is eat too much, drink too much, and make small talk at lunch," he said, adding that he had never missed anything or anyone important by swimming at noon.

If you take time out to relax and exercise every day, you'll rarely have to take time away from your goals because your energy level is running low. Of course, it's important to find exercise that you really enjoy. For me, it's a brisk daily walk, hiking and swimming as often as possible, and tennis when my travel schedule permits.

Also, find something enjoyable in the hard work you do every day. Wake up to inspiring music, and listen to a motivational tape on your way to work. Take frequent thinking and stretch breaks during the day. The brain retains more and functions most efficiently at the beginning and end of a work period. That means periodic breaks actually increase the amount you learn and accomplish. Breaks also make the work you do more satisfying because they divide your assignments into chunks, making it easier to see what you've done and how well you've done it.

Recently, I had an opportunity to interview five gold medal winners in the Olympic Decathlon: Bob Mathias, Milt Campbell, Bill Toomey, Rafer Johnson, and Bruce Jenner. While they were reminiscing over their Olympic triumphs, each as the greatest all-around athlete of his time, I was struck by the fact that it was a specific day, or meet, or event, or occurrence that was most vividly recalled by each man. If you think back over your own life, you'll find yourself remembering unique, especially rewarding moments, rather than the whole panorama.

When you view work as drudgery, it's difficult to produce those special days. You're expending a lot of effort just to overcome your own resistance. But when you love what you do, your energy naturally concentrates on your goals, maximizing the force of your efforts.

The best illustration of finding joy in hard work comes from a story first told by Edward Pulling, a great educator: In the Middle Ages, a courier went out to determine how laborers felt about their work. He went to a building site in France and approached the first construction worker and asked him to describe his job.

Angrily, the worker snapped, ''I'm cutting these impossible boulders with primitive tools and putting them together the way the boss tells me. I'm sweating under this blazing sun, it's backbreaking work, and it's boring me to death!''

The courier quickly backed off and turned to a second worker, only a few feet away, to ask the same question. ''What are you doing here today?''

The second worker smiled and lifted his arm to the sky. ''Can't you see? I'm building a magnificent cathedral!''

CHAPTER TEN

Flextactic: Find Goals That Benefit Yourself and Others

Performance Goals and Outcome Goals

Not too long ago I ran my first marathon—or I should say jogged, panted, shuffled, and groaned through my first marathon. I was inspired by my friend and colleague Harvey Mackay, author of *Swim with the Sharks* and *Sharkproof,* who attacks everything he does with total commitment. Of course, thousands of people run marathons every year, but Harvey and I hadn't even considered it until we were on the far side of fifty years of age. It wasn't so bad for Harvey, who's a fitness fanatic and keeps himself in great shape, but it was a major ordeal for me. My family have all been large-boned people, and large bones surround themselves with meat—nearly two hundred pounds of it in my case.

After I dragged myself across the finish line and recuperated for a month, I reluctantly agreed to run another marathon with Harvey Mackay. He and I had two different types of goals, however. Harvey's goal was to have the best time in our age bracket. My goal was to finish the race and better my previous result. I was running for internal satisfaction. He was running for internal satisfaction plus external results.

In order to achieve your life's objectives, it's extremely important to understand the differences between what I call Performance Goals and Outcome Goals. With Performance Goals, you compete against yourself, as I did by torturing myself to improve my time in the marathon. Outcome Goals are attained by competing against others, which is what Harvey Mackay does in marathons. He not only wants to become more fit, he also wants to win his age bracket.

I have a friend who was a moderately successful tennis player until the day he encountered a coach who taught him the correct way to serve. Up to that point, he had been able to get the ball into the service court with a fairly high degree of accuracy and power—enough to win many of his tournaments. The coach pointed out, however, that his form was wrong, and suggested that my friend make some adjustments. But of the first hundred balls he served in practice with the new technique, only two made it into the service court. The remainder slammed into the net, flew out of bounds, or sailed clear over the fence into the surrounding park. Over time, however, my friend became more accurate with the new method. He was amazed to find that he had far greater power than ever before, even though he had always thought of himself as having a strong first serve. The more he practiced and focused on the correct form, the more his performance improved.

Eventually he set a goal of getting 75 percent of his first serves into play. This was a Performance Goal of doing better than he had done in the past. As his accuracy and power improved, he began to become more competitive. He then set a goal of moving up to A-level competition and winning 75 percent of his tournaments, including a regional final. These were Outcome Goals, based on external results.

Your aspirations probably include a mix of Performance Goals and Outcome Goals. It's very important to recognize, however, that Outcome Goals necessarily introduce external factors over which you may have no control. There are environmental factors, and there are the other people you're competing with. These external factors can make the pursuit of your Outcome Goals very frustrating, and frustration is a waste of energy. But since the objective of goal setting is to make the most of your energy and your overall potential, I believe that Performance Goals are most effective. As much as possible, your goals should have you competing with yourself, not with someone else.

Competition: Winner or Loser?

Competition is the foundation of Outcome Goals. Highly competitive people don't necessarily care about their own inner satisfaction in doing a job well or in providing a service that must benefit others in order to be meaningful. Rather, they care most about the perception of themselves as superior, as "the winner." Excessively competitive individuals put a great deal of energy into manipulating other people's impressions, rather than building their own self-respect by working toward personally meaningful goals.

Extreme competitiveness can also get in the way of effective teamwork and cooperation, which are absolutes for survival in today's global economy. Overly competitive people are uncomfortable in team efforts, knowing that they'll have to share the glory of achievement rather than having it all to themselves. Their co-workers sense this, of course, and are reluctant to fully trust them.

Am I saying there's something inherently wrong with one cellular phone company or computer company competing with another? Absolutely not. Competition provides the soil in which free enterprise and democracy take root, and we all know what happens when a company or group has no competition. Seldom does lack of competition result in reasonable prices or great service. The problems come from the insatiable need for status and external reward that an overly competitive nature often fosters.

In our status-oriented culture, healthy competition to ensure quality, choice, and value can quickly give way to "knocking the other guy" in order to look good. An obsession with success at any price has often resulted in a distortion of basic values in many areas of life.

Social critics like the late Christopher Lasch, author of *The Culture of Narcissism,* and Aaron Stern, who wrote one of my favorite books, *Me: The Narcissistic American,* have observed that history's most successful societies have been those with a balance of interdependence and mutual support among all members. As societies become materially well-off, they tend to fall prey to self-indulgence, and the takers outnumber the givers. The takers have their feast, the givers get stuck with the check, and the price gets higher every decade.

Competition and the rewards that motivate it will always remain important elements in life, but, paradoxically, focusing on competition is often the worst way to compete. The CEO of one of America's most successful companies put it this way: "The successful individuals I know aren't interested in stepping on other people to get to the top. Their goal, instead, is to do such a good job that they become recognized as leaders in a fast field of excellent talent. In fact, the better your competitors do, the better you look by coming in first. The goal of any organization should be to assemble the most talented, best-trained, most highly motivated team in the industry, so that as a group you can all become first in the marketplace."

I once attended a high school basketball game in order to see an outstanding scorer who had received some attention in the local newspapers. He was by far the best player on his team. In fact, he was so far superior to his teammates that he scored virtually every basket. Perhaps he honestly felt this was his team's best chance for winning games, and it also showcased his abilities to visiting college recruiters. I certainly wasn't disappointed in the performance of this gifted athlete during the game I attended. As I recall, he scored more than fifty points. His team lost, however, as it did in every other game that season—and the star never did have a career as a college player, perhaps because he had grown used to playing basketball as if it were an individual sport.

Don't let one person dominate a group enterprise, no matter how gifted he or she may be, and don't try to take over such an enterprise yourself. You may look good for a moment, but you'll most likely look very bad in the end.

Goals for the Greater Good

Today there is a corporate revolution under way in this country, with businesses moving toward small, self-directed management teams in which maximum flexibility and synergy are encouraged. This kind of teamwork is not a really new concept, though it has been slow to gain acceptance in America, where independence and challenge to authority are central to our culture.

One individual who used the team approach to successfully reach his goals was James Cash Penney. The fabulous Mr. Penney, starting with a small store in Wyoming in 1902, built a multibillion-dollar business empire on one simple principle: The Golden Rule. In fact, the JC Penney stores were called "Golden Rule Stores" for many years, and it was Mr. Penney's personal faith in that rule—always treating the customer as he himself would want to be treated—that made the business grow and prosper.

Perhaps even more important than his customer-first policy was Penney's attitude toward his workforce. He never used the word *employee,* preferring to call all those working in his company his partners and associates. Penney devoted his life to treating them as he would want to be treated, knowing if he could help them earn a better living in a positive working environment, his own success would be assured. The late Sam Walton, who built the largest merchandising business in America in recent decades with his Wal-Mart stores, remembered J. C. Penney as one of his most inspiring role models.

Treat others as you would want to be treated. It sounds simple, doesn't it? But there are many hidden complications and temptations.

In particular, you should beware of what I call "utility traps." These are situations in which following your own self-interest in the short run hurts everyone's long-term success. Oil companies, lumber companies, and until recently, the U.S. automobile industry come to mind when we think of decisions for short-term gain versus long-term global consequences. Balancing individual goals with those serving the greater good is the only way to benefit everyone's basic interests. The longer I live, the more I realize that people who want to help themselves can do so only by benefiting others.

I recently came across a story that really moved me about just such an individual. It's the true account of a blind boy whose team effort changed the lives of millions of people in future generations. It is a story of sacrifice, courage, and frustration, filled with obstacles caused by jealous, self-serving adults who felt that allowing a young boy to succeed would threaten and diminish their own efforts.

Although he had perfect vision at his birth in the early

1800s, Louis Braille lost his eyesight as a young child playing with a sharp tool in his father's workshop. In those days blind children rarely were allowed to go to school. Most blind people became beggars, or remained totally dependent on their families.

Louis's parents, however, were determined to help him make something of his life. Although their friends thought they were unreasonably strict, his parents loved him enough to treat him as a normal child with plenty of responsibilities along with caring guidance. He was required to clean his room, help with the yard work, and dress himself, a task he finally mastered after months of trial and error.

A priest named Father Palluy took special interest in Louis and taught him history and science in private lessons at the local church. When the priest could no longer answer his questions, he made a special effort to arrange for Louis to be sent to a boarding school for the blind at the age of ten, where he would have an opportunity to learn to read.

Although conditions at the school were harsh and primitive, Louis Braille was a gifted student and even taught himself to play the piano. Reading, however, proved to be more difficult. Each letter of the alphabet was raised on the page so it could be read by touch, but the complex shapes of the letters meant that a single book often took several months to complete. The process was so slow that blind students forgot the words at the beginning of a sentence before they got to the end. The entire school library had only fourteen specially made books, because they were so difficult and expensive to produce, each one created by hand.

Louis's teacher told him that people had tried for many years to find a better way for the blind to read, and at the age of ten, Louis Braille made it his life goal to find a better way. He had heard his teacher talk about night writing, a technique used by soldiers to send messages in the dark. Each word was broken into sounds which were represented by a different pattern of raised dots, punched into paper by a stylus. Its inventor, a man named Captain Barbier, occasionally visited the school for the blind to help the students learn to use it.

Barbier's night-writing system required almost a hundred dots to write a simple word, and it was far too complicated for most of the blind students to use. Using an awl, the same kind of tool that had blinded him, Louis spent two years punching out paper in an attempt to create an improved reading system. Word soon spread outside the school that a better way to read was being created. Captain Barbier rushed to the school to meet the teacher who had streamlined his method and was outraged to discover that it was a boy of twelve. He wanted no part of the research and left the school in a huff, suggesting that the blind had diminished mental capabilities anyway, and he wasn't going to waste his valuable time observing the efforts of a demented child.

For three more years, Louis worked every night after school and every free day, including spring, summer, and winter breaks at home, trying to simplify his system. Everyone told him to give it up. For hundreds of years, brilliant older scientists and scholars had failed. Why not face the fact that handicapped people are destined to stay that way?

By the age of fifteen, Louis Braille had worked out a six-dot pattern, which he called a cell. He then numbered each dot in the cell, creating a different, simple pattern for each letter. He taught the system to all the boys in his dormitory, so they could take notes in class. When the headmaster called Louis in for a demonstration, he read back the principal's dictation word for word. But although the headmaster was astounded, no one would contribute any funds to produce new books with Louis's system. The school's benefactors were insulted by the idea that the books they had paid for in the past were now obsolete, and they weren't about to invest in a boy's dream. One wrote: "I have been giving you money to print books and now you tell me they are not good enough. You'll never get another cent from me!"

When Louis graduated from the school at nineteen, he was asked to stay on as a teacher. His salary was meager, though he was an expert in grammar, history, geography, math, and music. Since no one would help finance the creation of a library for the blind, Louis taught classes by day and worked through the night punching dots to make books, one at a time, for the blind students. Sacrificing his health for his cause, and lowering his resistance to disease by his grueling schedule, he contracted tuberculosis at the age of twenty-six.

During his convalescence and subsequent relapses, a new headmaster, Dr. Dufau, took over the leadership of the school and was shocked by the unorthodox methods and disquieting progress being made by the blind students with their classwork. As has happened so often throughout history, all of the books were burned, the tools destroyed, and the students forbidden to continue this nontraditional reading method.

In response, Louis Braille and the students formed an underground network. Late at night, the boys would use darning needles or nails to punch out the dots and create Braille's method to study from. When they were caught, they were beaten severely on the hands with wooden rulers and deprived of food. They continued nevertheless, until a new teacher approached the headmaster and pointed out to him that no amount of beatings and starvings·could hold back progress. Dufau could do what he liked to the students, but one day all blind people would be using this alphabet and his school would be left behind. Appealing to the headmaster's pride, the teacher said "Wouldn't you like to be known as the man who helped launch this unique method?"

This new slant on the problem flattered Dr. Dufau's competitive instinct. He loved being on the winning side of issues and he decided he could use Louis's dot system to attract attention, prestige, and money for himself and the school. Louis was put on stage in front of scientists, teachers, and government officials. Most of them thought it was a trick. Then two blind children were called up on stage. While one of the children was sent out of the room, a member of the audience read one page aloud from a randomly selected book. The blind child on the stage wrote down what was being read, using Louis Braille's dot system, and then the second child was brought back into the room and asked to read it. Brushing his fingers quickly and smoothly across the page of dots, the boy read it confidently and clearly. The audience instantly stood and cheered!

People from all over the world began asking for information on this new raised-dot alphabet for the blind, which they called the Braille system. A Braille printing press was designed and put into operation. Schools for the blind soon opened everywhere.

With his health continuing to deteriorate, Louis Braille continued punching out his books by hand for the students at the school. When he died at age thirty-five, he was still virtually unknown to the public. Not a single newspaper printed even a one-line obituary. Yet today he is known worldwide as the deliverer of one of the greatest gifts a nonsighted person can ever receive—the ability to read and learn through his raised-dot alphabet, fashioned by a crude tool, like the one in his father's workshop that had blinded him thirty-two years before at the age of three.

Louis Braille had a marvelous Performance Goal: to create a practical reading system for people like himself. It was not a competitive goal. He was competing with himself to find a better way to enjoy his passion for reading. He sacrificed his health and even his life to perfect a system that would help his students to read, an activity that most people take for granted.

As we set our Performance Goals, our Outcome Goals, our personal goals, and our team goals, we should remember those who have made life better and more meaningful for us. Even more important, we should seek to do as much for generations yet to come.

CHAPTER ELEVEN

Flextactic: Be Flexible in Your Expectations

Success Is a Self-fulfilling Prophecy

Focused, concentrated energy is your most important asset in achieving your goals. But this energy does not simply descend upon a certain number of fortunate people while missing others entirely. The fact is, maximizing the power of your energy and channeling it in the right direction is a function of your own self-expectations.

My first academic encounter with the power of expectations came from a professor in graduate school, S. I. Hayakawa, who, prior to becoming a U.S. senator, was best known for his theories on the "self-fulfilling prophecy." A self-fulfilling prophecy is a statement or belief that is objectively neither true nor false, but that becomes true as soon as it is believed. Because at a basic level the mind can't distinguish between something that is real and something that is vividly imagined, the concept of self-expectation is vitally important to an understanding of effective goal setting.

Research has demonstrated many times that the human body produces physiological reactions to all sorts of thoughts and emotions. What the mind harbors, the body manifests in biological response, and scientists have discovered that our brains release powerful hormones as a result of certain thoughts or expectations. Several of these hormones have been identified,

114

including enkephalin, beta-endorphin, and dynorphin. They are energy boosters and natural pain relievers many times more powerful than morphine.

Hormones play an important role in regulating certain of our biological processes. Adrenaline, for example, stimulates us to "fight or flight" in the presence of danger. A University of California research team made an interesting discovery that seemed to confirm earlier findings concerning these naturally produced chemicals. You are probably familiar with the "placebo effect," which takes its name from the Latin word *placebo*, meaning "I shall please." Placebos are neutral substances given to volunteers for comparison with experimental drugs. By measuring the difference in responses to the placebo and the drug being tested, psychological effects can be distinguished from biological ones.

The University of California study involved a group of volunteers who had just had their wisdom teeth extracted. Some of the subjects received morphine to alleviate their pain, while others received a placebo, which they believed to be morphine. Many of the placebo recipients said they experienced dramatic relief from their pain, but when a drug that blocks the effects of the naturally produced painkillers was given to them, the discomfort returned almost immediately. The test confirms a principle that is very important to goal achievement and to living a fulfilled life. When a placebo is given, and the individual believes he or she is getting relief, the brain releases chemical energy to confirm that belief. In other words, the placebo effect is triggered by self-expectation.

Positive Expectations for Yourself and Others

Clearly, one of the most important steps you can take toward achievement is to cultivate a high expectation for success. And it's equally important for you to expect success for other members of your inner circle, especially children.

Children rise to the expectations of the significant adult role models in their lives, and the home environment is by far the most significant factor in determining a child's success. The late Lawrence Kohlberg, the famous Harvard psychologist who studied child development, was fond of saying that positive values are "caught, not taught." That is, children are more likely to emotionally absorb their parents' values, rather than intellectually learn those values. Parents should teach by example.

Recently I read a news story that dramatically illustrates the impact of low parental expectations. Two young boys had been caught stealing handcuffs and other items from a police car. When the policeman asked them why they did it, the boys responded that their mother had always told them they would end up in jail eventually because they were always behaving badly. In fact, on the day of the theft their mother had reminded them again how bad they were and that they would eventually go to jail. She was correct, but perhaps she was also to blame.

While visiting Sea World in Florida, my grandchildren were amazed to see four-ton whales jumping out of the water and over a rope positioned ten feet above the surface. We learned from the trainers that they begin by placing a rope on the bottom of the pool and rewarding the whale when it passes over. Gradually the rope is raised until it is high above the water.

Just as animals can be conditioned to perform extraordinary feats, they can also be conditioned negatively. For example, there are the so-called "electronic fences" for keeping rambunctious dogs in the confines of their owners' yards. Wires are buried around the perimeter of the property and a battery collar is placed around the dog's neck. When the dog goes out of bounds, it receives a shock. After a few negative reinforcements, the dog knows better than to risk crossing the line. Even if the dog's collar is taken off and the buried wire is dug up and thrown away, the dog will still refrain from crossing the line. He has been conditioned to expect a certain outcome from his behavior, and he will continue to expect it regardless of the fact that external conditions may have changed.

People also become conditioned by successes and failures. They learn to perform at a level consistent with their expectations and the expectations that others have for them. Unfortunately, most perceived limits are the result of negative conditioning, and in fact there are no real boundaries to current or future achievements.

Just as the Sea World whales were encouraged through positive reinforcement, people respond to rewards, appreciation, recognition, and praise. Unlike animals, however, we have the power to control the conditioning of our lives and the lives of those close to us. Let me share with you some qualities that can foster positive expectations in any group situation, whether in business or in a home:

- There is emphasis on building the self-worth and self-respect of each individual.
- Each member respects the needs, dignity, and individuality of every other member.
- Relationships are characterized by loving, caring, trust, and affection.
- The group is secure and cohesive, with pride in its members and their accomplishments. There is a feeling of ownership and opportunities for involvement and participation in the group's affairs.
- Faultfinding, bickering, and quarreling are kept to a min-

imum. Differences are settled reasonably, fairly, and amicably.

- Communications are free and open. People are encouraged to express their opinions and feelings without fear of recrimination or reprisal.
- Expectations for each member of the group are high and positive, and there is cooperative effort to help each person achieve his or her goals.

How the Half-Empty Glass Becomes Half-Full

Psychologist Robert Kriegel conducted a program for sales executives in a management training business which had been suffering from the effects of a tight economy. In his book, *The C Zone*, which he co-authored with his wife and which deals with performance under pressure, he describes two different people dealing with the same problem.

Louis, the first of Kriegel's subjects, was in the biggest slump of his career. "Everybody's cut their training budgets," he complained, "and a lot of the programs I sold are being canceled. There's just no money around. The way I'm being avoided, I feel like I'm peddling a communicable disease. It's gotten to the point that I'm not even making calls."

But Charlene, the second subject, had gone 25 percent over her quota for the previous quarter. She said, "I know the economy is tight and budgets for our programs are being cut, but some people are still buying. I've just got to work harder to find them. Actually, the economy has helped me in a way. There's less competition because a lot of companies in the field have laid people off. So when I do find someone who is interested, I usually get the order. I've actually opened quite a few new accounts.''

The difference between the two responses is like night and day. The economy didn't cause Louis to fail and Charlene to succeed. Self-expectation did! And with Charlene's attitude of self-expectation comes the flexibility to look at setbacks not as obstacles to overcome but as opportunities to expand—truly the mind-set of a twenty-first-century goal setter.

All this reminds me of an interesting day I once had on a ski slope in Aspen, Colorado. I was just learning to ski, and I'd mistakenly taken the chairlift to the top of a ski run marked with a black diamond symbol, indicating that this run was for expert skiers. Even though I was just a beginner, I smiled and began to fantasize that I was just an Olympic champion about to rocket down the slopes. But in less than a minute my initial self-expectation of confidently traversing moguls and steep inclines at exhilarating speeds quickly gave way to stark terror. I was soon imagining a fractured fibula, a possible broken neck, or perhaps a tree implanted in some part of my body that didn't need one.

Dr. Kriegel says that most of us believe that our attitudes are caused by what we actually see before us, which in my case was an almost vertical drop. Some people get the same anxiety when they stand up to speak at a meeting. They think it's caused by actually seeing the size of the audience. But according to Kriegel, this is not the case. It's much more likely that I was already thinking about taking that steep run while I was riding up the chairlift. It was then, before I even saw the slope, that I started to feel anxious and my heart began to beat faster. By the time I got off the chair at the top of the run, I was already a basket case. Similarly, most nervous public speakers start feeling anxious when they first find out they are going to speak at a meeting.

What we see in front of us, then, is not what's actually there, but what is being constructed for us by our attitudes and expectations. With this in mind, let me introduce three foundations for building a positive self-expectation goal-setting program:

1. A well-constructed goals program moves from one realizable goal to another, always building on the previous success to meet the next challenge.

By breaking down obstacles into smaller parts that can be handled successfully, you can experience a series of successes, which become a self-renewing cycle. Each success leads to confident self-expectations and those, in turn, lead to new successes. Instead of a "vicious circle," in which one problem gives way to another, a succession of positive accomplishments creates a "victor's circle," in which one success leads to further successes.

Albert Bandura, a professor at Stanford University, is one of the most important figures in motivational psychology. Dr. Bandura has found that self-expectation, "the feeling that one can perform successfully," is one of the strongest motivating factors in all areas of human achievement. When a person is hungry for a meal and satisfies that need by eating, the person is no longer hungry; but when you believe you can achieve your goals and do in fact reach one, the motivation to continue upward to bigger and better achievements is strengthened by the feeling of accomplishment, not lessened by it. When a basketball player gets a "hot hand" by making a couple of three-pointers in a row, he or she seems to gain momentum on those early successes. Reinforce yourself positively while you are in the process of achieving your daily goals. This is something that an athlete, an entertainer, or any other professional does when performance is going well.

A strong record of success can provide another boost to

self-expectation. This is the confidence that comes from having successfully met similar challenges in the past. When most people slide behind the steering wheel of their cars, they don't wonder about their chances of successfully driving to their desired destination. They have driven enough to have faith in their own ability. The more we accomplish, the more we realize that we have been endowed with great capacity for achievement. Often this capacity lies dormant within us, and only by exercising it can we come to appreciate just how remarkable it really is.

2. Keep your goals tangible and specific, so that you can point to specific accomplishments.

In this way, your self-expectation will keep a high standard constantly before you, challenging you to meet your own aims. Just as the computer on your desk needs factual input, your mental computer needs specific information about your goals. This is particularly true in today's customer-driven business world, where quality, innovation, convenience, and choice are the keys to success.

The 7-Eleven Japan Company provides a good example of how twenty-first-century achievers must learn to think. The Japanese firm bought the franchise rights to 7-Eleven from Dallas-based Southland Corporation. By 1990, the franchisee was doing so well that it bought 70 percent of the American parent company for $430 million. How can a franchisee buy the franchiser? By getting very specific about its business goals!

Three days a week, President Toshifumi Suzuki and some twenty top management people sit in their well-appointed boardroom for a lunch of the instant noodles, prepackaged sandwiches, and snacks that they hope to sell in their 4,809-store chain. It's a spot check of what's on the shelves. One stale rice ball and that brand is history. ''I won't sell what I wouldn't eat,'' says Suzuki.

Backed by one of the most sophisticated product-tracking

systems in the world, 7-Eleven Japan is completely tuned in to providing what customers want. Its 42 percent operating profit margin far outshines its competitors. The company has installed a $200-million system that monitors inventory and tracks customer preferences. Clerks even key in the sex and approximate age of each customer to monitor buying patterns. Orders are transmitted instantly via satellite to distribution centers and manufacturers. Anything that doesn't move immediately is discontinued. Of the three thousand items each Japanese franchisee carries, 70 percent are replaced annually. A bare-bones inventory saves money and energy, with shelf space allocated only to what shoppers are really buying.

"American convenience stores," says Suzuki, "spend too much time trying to act like supermarkets—carrying too broad a line to be responsive or profitable. Today, in a rapidly changing economy, you have to know what you're doing every day and be prepared at a moment's notice to meet a sophisticated customer's new demands."

Apply the strategy of this successful retailer to your own goals program. You need to do your homework. You need to access the potential market for your goals. You need to have concrete, trackable daily goals that match your life-forming objectives. And like 7-Eleven Japan, you need to be prepared to change course to meet a sophisticated *world's* new demands.

I've written my major goals on a Priority Goal Card I keep with my daily time-management planner. I take these Goal Cards with me wherever I go and refer to them several times daily. By doing this whenever you're faced with a decision, you can determine whether a choice will help or hinder the achievement of your paramount life goals. Ask yourself often: Do I feel good about my progress to date? Why or why not? Am I going where I want to go, doing what I want to do, and becoming who I want to become? What do I need to stay on track to achieve the goals

I've set for myself? Clear, positive answers to these questions will magnify your energy and motivation to move forward.

3. Use your goals to preempt expectations others might set for you.

With a set of tangible goals, you're controlling the expectations, and you're focusing energy where you want it to go. Let your own realistic but challenging expectations be your primary guide. When you do seek external feedback on your progress toward your goals, be sure it is from people who are truly interested in seeing you succeed. Don't seek feedback from fairweather friends, competitive peers, or any person who doesn't have your best interests at heart. Neutral doesn't count. Get feedback from someone who is on your side but who will also be objective and honest with you.

Time and again, I've observed that misery truly does love company. And jealousy makes for some of the most miserable people I know. Surpass the achievements of your particular social crowd or your business colleagues, and look out for the slings and arrows of the many who wish you were back where they are. This can often be quite subtle. The authoritarian manager, who supports you and comforts you when you're down, may like you best when you are in just that dependent condition. When you start succeeding beyond his expectations and comfort level, he may be among the first ones urging you to back off, to limit your horizons, and to lower your goals.

Ultimately nobody else is responsible for your life but you. Nobody else is accountable for your actions. Therefore, nobody's expectations for you and opinions about you are as important as your own.

Whether or not you are aware of it, you have a running conversation with yourself from the time you get up to the time you go to sleep. Your thoughts and ideas are talking to you, telling you what to expect. Most people make the mistake of expressing their expectations in negative terms: A tennis player may set a goal of not double-faulting, or an employee may set a goal of not being late so often. This negativity reflects a fundamental misunderstanding of how the mind works. The human mind can't focus on the reverse of an expectation or idea. The words "double fault" remind the tennis player of the condition he wants to avoid. "Being late" reminds the employee of the problem, not the solution. When we think we need to lose weight, our minds store the self-image of being too heavy. It is extremely difficult, if not impossible, to concentrate on not being upset. It's the same thing as saying, "Don't make mistakes." The mind always moves you *toward* your dominant thought.

Successful people tell themselves over and over again that they are in the process of winning personal victories and achieving important life goals. When you are positive and constructive in your self-talk, your self-image rises to meet your expectations. This is especially important after the completion of a performance or a project. Confirm to yourself that you have completed the task, and affirm to yourself that you are a winner, a person on the way to achieving your goals. Evaluate your performance, and applaud the things you did well. Be aware of the mistakes you made, learn from them, but don't dwell on them.

Without exception, the real achievers in any field accept their uniqueness, affirm their positive qualities and accomplishments, and have increasingly high, positive expectations for themselves and those close to them. They expect the very best from themselves and from others as well.

When you hold yourself in high regard, it's much easier to think well of everyone.

When you are able to applaud yourself, it's much easier to applaud others.

When you see yourself as an achiever, it's much easier to recognize other achievers and encourage them to win.

From time to time your performance may fall just short of your goals. But you will never, in the long run, rise above your expectations.

CHAPTER TWELVE

Flextactic: Set New Standards When You Exceed Your Goals

When the End of the Rainbow Comes Too Soon

Goals should always be the means, not the end. Goals are like stepping-stones to the stars. They should never have the effect of limiting achievement or narrowing horizons. But unfortunately, they sometimes have that limiting effect.

In my work with Olympic and professional athletes, I've met many individuals whose major lifetime goal was winning a gold medal or playing in the Super Bowl, the World Series, or the NBA Championship. But once they reached that goal, or something near it, they had nowhere to go. It was all downhill from that point—and I don't mean that life was an easy ride in neutral, either; it was more like a roller-coaster plunge into a valley of despair. Can you imagine the effects of reaching your ultimate goal before you were twenty-five or thirty years of age? Or, in the case of many Olympians, before you were twenty?

Discovering new, ever more meaningful goals is a lifelong challenge. For many athletes, this problem remains forever unsolved; they find themselves spiritually and psychologically adrift, fixated on trophies, medals, and press clippings from the past.

Nor is this syndrome limited to sports stars. I know a business executive whose major goal was to become financially independent by the age of forty and then retire and play golf. He reached that goal but became extremely bored after a year of playing golf every day. Fortunately, he recognized the problem and found a solution. He went back to college, earned a degree in a completely different field, and today is happily engaged in a career as an environmental engineer.

Traditionally, many people have had a goal of "lifetime security" in a permanent job. That may have been reasonable twenty years ago or even ten years ago, but it is almost impossible today, with the exception of a few positions in the government. Even military service, which used to be a sure ticket to a pension, is now vulnerable. How many more bases will close? How large an army and navy do we really need? Which types of aircraft will survive? Instead of aspiring to lifetime security, flexible achievers focus on being well qualified in as many areas as possible for a challenging, always evolving career. Staying well qualified means ensuring that goals don't become dead ends or stopping points. It means being able to set new standards when you achieve your current goals.

"The Road to Heaven . . ."

Once you create and follow a really good goal-setting program, you'll probably find that you're not just meeting, but exceeding your expectations. And if you're making effective use of the flextactics approach, you'll always be able to set new standards and discover new possibilities when you've reached or exceeded your major goals.

As this process takes place, you must learn to balance two distinct but important elements of a fulfilling life. First, it's important to take satisfaction in your achievements, to enjoy your success, and to "smell the roses" every day. But it's just as important to remember that the real joy of achievement is in the challenge, not in the accomplishment. Even in a rapidly changing world, the wisdom of the ages never changes: "The road to heaven is heaven itself."

Life is based on growth and finding new challenges to face and overcome, new contributions to make to society, and constantly coming to a better understanding of yourself and the universe in which you live. "Taking satisfaction in your achievements" is to "looking for new challenges" as "relaxation and exercise" is to "hard work." There is no better feeling than the joy of knowing that your personal efforts are making a creative contribution to the overall quality of human life.

In theory, it would seem that once you've reached a major life goal, you would no longer be as highly motivated to set future goals. If, for example, you needed venture capital to launch your new business, you wouldn't keep looking for new investors once you've raised a sufficient amount of money. But self-expectation is the exception. Self-expectation not only empowers you to strive for your objectives, it continues to motivate you even after you've reached your initial goal. Once we believe we can meet a major challenge successfully, we find that our motivation to achieve has been strengthened rather than diminished by this feeling.

Golda Meir, the former prime minister of Israel, was known for her vision and wisdom. She was a shopkeeper's daughter who attended school in the fortresslike building on Fourth Street near Milwaukee's famous Schlitz brewing factory. Speaking only broken English after immigrating from Europe, this plain, nondescript child was late for school almost every day because of the chores she had to do at home. But brilliant, courageous, and persistent, she became one of the most respected world leaders of the twentieth century. At the age of seventy-one, while serving as prime minister, she returned to Milwaukee and her school. It had been fifty-one years since she left the United States.

She told the inner-city youth at her old school that she had been born into a minority environment and had lived only slightly above the poverty level. She also told the children, "When you're young, it isn't really important to decide exactly what you want to become when you grow up. It is much more important to decide on the way you want to live." Golda Meir spoke of service rather than material reward, and of destiny rather than money.

On the corporate level, the experience of IBM in the early 1990s is a good illustration of the need to focus on the journey of constant growth, creativity, and quality, rather than on the destination as represented by the bottom line of a financial statement. Throughout the entire postwar period, IBM had been the model of a supremely successful American corporation. For years the company seemed like an invincible army of highly disciplined workers in white shirts and narrow ties. But that very aura of discipline was beginning to undermine initiative and creativity. Despite huge cash reserves and a stock price that never seemed to fall below a hundred dollars, the company had developed a "don't rock the boat" philosophy—at a time when the boat was rocking very fast in the computer industry. IBM was no longer a comfortable environment for aggressive individuals like Ross Perot, who quit after meeting his yearly sales quota at the end of January and being told he couldn't sell any more computers for the rest of the year. IBM's reliance on big mainframe computers, and its failure to anticipate the importance of desktop and laptop machines, almost destroyed the company and brought about radical restructuring in the 1990s that eliminated thousands of jobs.

A bottom line solidly in the black always looks good on an annual report, but those numbers say nothing about the sense of creativity, risk taking, and adventure that's present in a company. If those qualities aren't encouraged, even a juggernaut like IBM will be humbled.

Yes, dinosaurs ruled the earth, but they sure don't rule it anymore.

The Art of Collecting Minutes

Success, then, is not something to be possessed. Rather, it is the ongoing process of becoming all we can and should be. We must remember that success has little direct connection with money, although there is nothing wrong with being a rich success. Some rich people are extremely successful, and others are not.

Success is not your personal ''score'' in life, although there is nothing wrong with putting plenty of points on the board when you can do it fair and square. Beware, however, of the idea that to be a real success you must ''outscore'' everyone else. If you measure your success only by what you buy or produce, you are doomed to eternal dissatisfaction. There is always someone who can buy more or produce faster. There is always someone younger, better-looking, more popular, quicker, smarter, and stronger. Whenever you use any type of material measuring stick, success will always remain just beyond your fingertips.

To say ''I am a success'' is to attach some kind of permanence to the word, as if nothing will ever change, as if the world will always be the way it is now. But things don't stay the same. Time and energy are always in motion. The global market shifts on a daily basis. Interest rates fluctuate. Everything is in flux, and especially everything involving human beings. When Robert Redford, some years ago, was named the top

American motion-picture box-office drawing card, he told a TV interviewer that his ambition had always been to reach the top, and that to be the best, he had to avoid being seduced by fame. Today, he has embraced the highly worthwhile goal of helping aspiring film producers create films with a positive message for society.

Very often, people who are deeply dissatisfied with their lives are those who allow their happiness to be put off until some imaginary point in the future. They are continually let down and frustrated. They're always waiting for some goal to be achieved or for some problem to be solved before they can feel any sense of accomplishment.

They might, for example, be waiting until:

- they get a better job
- the government changes its policies toward them
- they have more savings
- they buy a new home
- they graduate
- they get married or remarried
- the kids finish school and leave home
- they retire

If the condition of being happy cannot be experienced in the present moment, it will probably never be experienced at all. You cannot defer happiness pending some future occurrence, because the future is always uncertain. Some new challenge will always come along just as you find a solution to the previous one. Life is really a succession of problems and goals, both large and small, but genuine achievers are able to see these apparent obstacles for what they really are: endless opportunities for continued motivation and growth.

In an interview in *Parade* magazine, Norman Lear, the creator of some of America's most popular television series, reflected on his own concepts of success and fulfillment. He said, "Throughout the American scene—television, sports, government, and business—the message seems to be that life is made up of winners and losers. If you are not number one or in the top five, you've failed. There doesn't seem to be any reward for living up to your own potential and meeting or exceeding your own, personal expectations."

Then Lear continued, "To me, success is simply how you collect your minutes. You might spend millions of minutes to reach one goal. Then you spend a few thousand minutes, or a few hundred minutes, or maybe just one or two minutes enjoying it. If you are unhappy through those millions of minutes of achieving, what good are those fewer minutes of triumph? It doesn't equate. Happiness means taking pleasure in life's daily small successes. That's the most important thing I've learned in all my life."

Price Does Not Equal Value

Many of today's executives could benefit from what Norman Lear has to say. These are people with corner offices overlooking magnificent city skylines, but they never seem to look out their windows. They remain caught up in a large-scale game of Monopoly, trying to figure out how much is enough and how to stay on top. I know several top businesspeople who own fabulous homes in the country or near the ocean, but they go home only to eat and sleep. They've worked hard to have those vistas outside their windows, but they rarely enjoy them.

There are people who work six days a week to provide better lives for their children, yet one day they awaken to find that their children are gone and now have children of their own.

Others wait thirty years before taking a real vacation, only to discover that they have lost the ability to enjoy themselves.

As the undisputed world leader in many industries, Japan has a per capita income among the highest in the world. But what about quality of life? In recent years, several lawsuits filed in Japan by widows of business executives have been based upon the term *karoshi*, which means "working oneself to death." The longer a Japanese executive stays at the office, and the more pressure he places on himself, the more he is held in "esteem" by his company. But what kind of reward is that, when an urn of ashes is presented to his relatives? The Japanese call their living conditions *manuke*, which means "we lack three things"—time, space, and private lives.

The secret to avoiding goal-achievement "burnout" is the ability to enjoy both the rewards you've earned and the efforts involved in attaining them. At every stage of life, successful individuals are able to look back and reflect, "I've enjoyed every mile and every day of the journey in some way to this point." Unsuccessful individuals bitterly complain, "I've worked myself to the bone, and now I'm too tired and don't have enough time or money to enjoy the fruits of my labors. Is this all there is? I hope the great beyond is better than life here on earth!"

Perhaps the greatest failure of our time, up to this point, is to equate achievement solely with material possessions. So much of our time, energy, and resources is spent in an attempt to gain the outward trappings of achievement—to proclaim, "I've arrived!" to the world. Yet a concentration of status symbols really suggests that the owner is void of inner purpose and lacking in self-esteem.

Please don't misunderstand. I am very much in favor of purchasing items of quality and fine workmanship, because they last and because they function properly and safely. But I see little point in high price tags for their own sake. Oscar Wilde once defined a cynic as "someone who knows the price of everything and the value of nothing.'' Value is something quite different from price. The toys and trappings of affluence tell nothing about how important a person truly is. The true value of a person is measured by other criteria, such as integrity, generosity, and lasting contribution to the general good. It's interesting to note that the largest gifts ever made to sponsor New York's Lincoln Center, the Metropolitan Opera, and many of our finest universities and medical schools have come from anonymous donors.

Ask yourself right now: How fast am I spending my time and energy? On what am I spending them? Will this problem really matter in five years, or ten years, or fifty years? Most important, is this activity moving me toward achieving my life-forming goals?

Turn off the dim lights of unfocused, nondirectional energy. Instead, let the flextactics we've discussed transform your mind into a laserlike energy source of flexibility and focus. When goals are focused and in progression, they ignite a spark in the human mind with awesome creativity. When energy waves are concentrated and synchronized, they produce a beam of pure light with power enough to illuminate the universe.

CHAPTER THIRTEEN

Flextactics in Action: Putting Theory into Practice

Putting Theory into Practice

Let's review the flextactics we've introduced, and reinforce their key principles with real-life illustrations to help you make the new dynamics of goal setting an integral part of your personal and professional life.

Remember, your life-forming goals should be written on the first page of your journal. Each of the flextactics should be written on the second page, along with a few practical reminders and definitions to accompany each one. As you review the flextactics daily and weekly, consciously think of ways to incorporate them into your routine at work and at home, and give yourself credit as you become more adept at using them in your decision-making and goal-achievement programs. At the end of this book, you'll find a twenty-one-day plan to help you put everything we've covered into action.

Make Flexibility the Key to your Success

Throughout nature, there are two attributes of living things that seem to bode well for long-term survival. One is smallness of size, and the other is an ability to adapt well to changing circumstances. Dinosaurs may have ruled the earth for an age or two, but eventually they disappeared once and for all. They were replaced by smaller, smarter, more flexible animals who may not have been as physically powerful as a *T-rex*, but who were much more adaptable. In a similar way, vast corporations—railroads, phone companies, airlines, steelmakers—dominated the American economy while market conditions were suited to them, but those days are becoming a memory. In the new economy that's now emerging, you simply must be able to chart your own destiny, and you should rejoice in the chance to do so. Lifetime employment by a paternalistic company, including benefits and a retirement plan, just isn't going to happen anymore on the scale we've known since 1945. We can lament this change all we want, but it will keep coming nonetheless.

I suggest there are great opportunities at this moment in time. Throughout much of its history, America was a nation built on small-scale, individual initiative. At the Smithsonian Institution in Washington, D.C., thousands of patented inventions are on display, each one lovingly crafted by an American worker who had an idea. These were people who really believed they could make a difference. They weren't just writing memos to their supervisors; they were taking action on their own to turn their dreams into realities. We may have lost that kind of initiative over the past few decades—perhaps our dreams have been getting smaller, perhaps we've stopped having dreams at all—but from now on there's going to be a lot less importance attached to corner offices and corporate memberships at the country club and a lot more focus on "every man for himself." I don't mean to sound insensitive, and I know some painful readjustments will be needed, but in many ways I'm glad to see this change. All the tools you need for success—the educational resources, the powerful technologies that can put the world at your fingertips—are within your reach. Ask yourself: What can I do to take advantage of the vast transformations that are now taking place? What adjustments should I be making right now?

What do I have to offer the world? What are my dreams? And more important, what am I going to do with them?

Learn to Thrive on Risk

Accept change as a constant in today's world. Expect it. Welcome it. Recognize that large companies and traditional industries can no longer guarantee permanent employment or career security. Take advantage of the fact that smaller, rapidly growing, highly flexible, entrepreneurial companies are creating most of the new jobs.

There's an old saying, "If it ain't broke, don't fix it." This means that if you're successful for the time being, you should just keep doing more of the same thing in the future—but this is very dangerous thinking as we approach the twenty-first century. The new reality is "If it ain't broke, it's obsolete!" To survive and move ahead in today's volatile world you need to continually change your assumptions, upgrade your skills, and become more adaptable and resilient to the reality of constant change.

Even if you never own your own company or business, you must behave as if you're self-employed for the rest of your life. If you're currently working for someone else, never confuse your personal long-term interests with those of your employer. Set up your own training department and make sure the most important employee—*yourself*—is continuously updating his or her skills and education.

As vice president of software development at Data General Corporation, Bill Foster had an enviable position. While still in his early thirties, Foster was earning a hundred thousand dollars a year, and in a few more years his invested stock options would be worth nearly a million dollars. Yet he left behind the stock options and the cushy job to take a very big risk.

"I'd been hemming and hawing about quitting for years," Foster said. His desire to start a business began in the late 1970s.

On a family vacation, Foster took along a notebook, planning to spend the week working up some ideas. He got a tan, but he wrote not a single word. "I got home and said to myself, 'Ah, you're too old. Just forget it. Just be happy with what you're doing.' "

A year later, at two o'clock in the morning while Foster was on a business trip, the idea of striking out on his own suddenly reinvented itself. Awakened by the thought that he was going to quit his job and start his own company, Foster reached for his notebook and started writing down ideas. He outlined a business plan, and he made some notes about sources for financial backing. The next morning he called his wife and said, "Honey, when I get back, I'm going to quit."

Two weeks later Foster was no longer an employee of Data General. His former colleagues thought he was crazy. A friend took him sailing to tell him many people were convinced he'd been fired. They couldn't imagine that he would just get up and leave.

Foster said he left because trying to build his own company while still working for his former employer would have been too complicated, and unethical as well. He had a year's salary saved up. Though he had only the barest outline for his new business, he had his dream, and he was willing to risk his present security to pursue it.

He had decided to enter the field of "fault-tolerant" computers, whose software allows them to preserve data even during power outages.

Bill Foster knew a great deal about computers, but somewhat less about marketing. He didn't fully understand the difference between simply *having* an idea and *selling* the idea. In reality, the difference is like night and day. Foster had naively presumed that there was a lot of money out there and someone would be eager to invest in him.

At the end of his first year of going it alone, Foster wasn't exactly eager to attend any Christmas parties. He said, "I didn't want to see all those people who were still working, and who still had money coming in. I was withdrawing money from my savings every week, and it was a strange feeling. Having been conditioned to save and put money away, I never realized how I would react to taking it out. It was a very depressing experience. I was starting to believe some of the people who told me I'd made a big mistake."

Fighting off doubts, Foster worked with an energy and conviction he had never experienced before. He learned to follow up on every venture-capital lead and to talk to everyone who would listen. Whenever he read a magazine article about someone who had started a company, he immediately called the person to set up a meeting. He was amazed how much everyone liked talking about what they had done, and how willing they were to share their business plans, which Foster then used to refine his own.

Still desperate for funding, Foster arranged an appointment with a bank, but when he arrived he was informed that the appointment had been canceled. Now Foster not only needed funding, he needed some solace and encouragement. He decided to stop by the office of Robert Freiburghouse, a friend who owned a small software company. At the end of their conversation, Foster left a copy of the business plan that he had brought along for his bank appointment. "Bob Freiburghouse called me that same evening," Foster said, "and told me that my idea was better than what he was doing. He said, 'How would you like to have a partner?' "

Freiburghouse took charge of software development, and eventually capital was raised. The new company, called Stratus, opened for business in mid-1980. Five years later, it was generating revenues of over $80 million.

Foster said the most important element in his success was willingness to take risk without worrying about failing. He said,

"I guess I finally woke up to the fact that it didn't matter if I failed, and that fear was the worst reason in the world not to try. I don't consider myself a special person. When I was a kid I was an underachiever. No one really had very big expectations for me. I'm not smarter than other people. I don't have very clever ideas. But if you ask, 'Why don't people act on their dreams?' my answer is that most people don't like to take chances. But what's really at risk is ego—it's rarely a matter of life and death. Can your ego accept failure and can your mind stay focused on your dream? These are the questions that you must ask yourself."

I agree, and if you can answer yes, then *thrive on risk as a part of life.*

Use Your Past to Chart Your Future

Ask yourself, "If there were no constraints of money, time, or circumstance, what would I begin doing tomorrow?"

In order to answer that important question, use these other key questions as guides:

1. What did you love to do as a child?
2. Are you doing what you enjoy doing now in your personal and professional life and using your talents fully?
3. Are you making a contribution to the world and to other people that gives you a feeling of self-respect?

In 1940, at the age of eight, Dave Thomas dreamed that one day he would own the best restaurant in the world. All the customers would love his food and all the employees would do everything they were supposed to do. Most important, everyone would think he was a good boss, and every day when he walked into the restaurant people would be glad to see him.

Dave Thomas is now a millionaire many times over because he used his vivid imagination in childhood to create his life-forming goals. When he dreamed that dream at the age of eight, and visualized what the future would look like, he had no idea that his goal of a hamburger restaurant in Columbus, Ohio, would multiply into more than four thousand family restaurants throughout the country, all named after his daughter—Wendy.

Even if you're not pursuing your childhood aspirations today, it's still important to think back to what you loved to do and what talents you displayed at an early age. Remember to identify your personal character strengths, your natural abilities, educational experiences that may have brought you special knowledge and skills, and the names of people who are your primary personal network of role models and mentors. By writing all this in your journal, you can create a detailed self-assessment to help you design your major goals. You can give real meaning to the phrase ''Back to the Future!''

Make Your Life an Open Book

''Know thyself'' is one of the fundamental ideas of Western philosophy. In order to describe what you should be accomplishing with your journal, I would amend this maxim just slightly, to read: ''Know *everything good* about yourself!'' Make sure you've identified your talents and abilities, and the traits of character that distinguish you as a peak performer. Find out the names of people who can help you strengthen areas of weakness, and create a plan for getting in touch with these ''sounding boards'' and ''springboards.'' Put all this in your journal—really make your life and your dreams an open book—and then turn the journal entries into letters, faxes, e-mails, proposals, applications . . . and actions!

Use the Power of Visualization

I'm a great believer in honesty and in speaking from the heart. But there are times—especially in highly stressful business situations—when it can be useful to create a bit of distance between how you behave and how you might be feeling inside. Instead of immediately responding to the emotions churning within you, you may want to create a vision of how someone you admire might respond, and then model your behavior on that person. This is not the same thing as denying your own feelings. It's merely suppressing them for a while in order to gain a tactical advantage.

Bill Shoemaker was one of the greatest jockeys of all time, but he once committed one of the biggest mistakes a Thoroughbred rider can possibly make. In the 1957 Kentucky Derby, Shoemaker was riding Gallant Man, the favorite, when he misjudged the position of the finish line and momentarily pulled up his horse, who at that moment was nose to nose with the eventual winner, Iron Liege. Observers of the Derby had no doubt that Shoemaker's error was the cause of Gallant Man's defeat. When the jockey was questioned about the incident by officials after the race, Shoemaker at first suggested that Gallant Man had suddenly been frightened by a shadow, but under continued questioning he soon admitted his error.

The real test, however, would come when Shoemaker had to confront John Nerud, Gallant Man's trainer, who was essentially Shoemaker's boss. Years later, Nerud would recall, "All I wanted Shoemaker to say was that he'd made a mistake. If he said something about the horse being frightened by a shadow, I was going to hit him with a pair of binoculars."

Walking out of the jockey quarters, Shoemaker saw Nerud. The jockey approached and said simply, "I'm sorry. I made a mistake."

By not making excuses and by taking full responsibility for what had happened, Shoemaker behaved like a true champion. But it couldn't have been easy. In that situation, temptations abound, and in fact, Shoemaker's first explanation had been to blame external circumstances—but when it counted he took the heat himself.[8]

The next time you make the biggest mistake that could possibly be made—or what seems like it—remember this story of a great athlete who stumbled in front of millions of people and who then had the courage to admit it. Use this example, or any other example that similarly inspires you, as a vision to guide your own behavior, no matter how you may feel inwardly. And you'll find that once you start acting like a champion, you'll start feeling like one as well.

Create a Blueprint for Success

You are the world's greatest expert on yourself. There simply isn't any doubt about it—no one knows more about your hopes and your dreams and your fears and your foibles than you yourself. In your secret heart, your goals are quite clearly defined, and most likely they have been since your childhood. That doesn't mean, however, that you won't choose to delude yourself about them. All of us feel the pressure of what we believe the world expects us to do and to be, and under that pressure most of us feel the need to compromise on what we really want from life. This is part of growing up, and it's inevitable. But the danger arises when we convince ourselves that growing up means not just adjusting, but abandoning what we really want and need.

Why does this abandonment take place? It happens because we don't take a practical approach to realizing our most closely held wishes. We've already talked about the importance of using the past to chart the future and the importance of visualization in that process. But *creating a blueprint* is something quite different. Creating a blueprint means thinking of your dreams in very realistic terms. If you want to be a filmmaker, for example, it means learning the ins and outs of the industry you want to enter, reading up on the careers of outstanding directors and studio executives, deciding what schools to attend and what jobs to seek. You should certainly compose an imaginary Oscar acceptance speech in addition to all this, but don't let the beautiful dream distract you from the businesslike realities. Dessert is great, but it's still important to eat your vegetables!

If you don't take a practical approach to achieving your goals, sooner or later you'll start doubting yourself. You'll start beating yourself up for your pie-in-the-sky dreams, and you'll start settling for less than you really want because you don't clearly see how anything more is possible.

While I was a naval officer in Washington, D.C., after the Korean War, I conducted a study of Chinese interrogation methods. These methods were designed to separate and identify any captured Americans who could be turned into collaborators or informers, and I discovered that it had been relatively easy for the Chinese to separate strong-willed leaders among their prisoners from purposeless followers. The interrogation appeared simple and nonthreatening: Where are you from? Do you have a girlfriend back home? What are you fighting for? What are you going to do when you return home? What kind of career would you like most? What are you planning to study? How much money do you need? What is your favorite sports team? What is your religion?

Soldiers and airmen who gave specific, practical answers were classified as goal-oriented potential leaders. They were placed in maximum-security camps, were deprived of adequate food and shelter, and were tortured in an attempt to break their resolve. But Americans who gave vague answers about their lives and their future plans were recognized as ideal subjects for indoctrination. They were put in minimum-security camps that were almost like country clubs, with no machine-gun towers, no barbed-wire fences, no guard dogs. Instead, there were comfortable barracks, cafeterias, and recreation areas. Most important of all, there were study halls for reading Communist propaganda.

Though the prisoners in the maximum-security camps were beaten, starved, and forced to live in cages like animals, some prisoners from these camps escaped and got back to friendly territory. In contrast, no one escaped or even attempted to escape from the minimum-security country clubs. And yet, incredibly, despite superior food, shelter, clothing, and medical care, death and disease rates were many times higher than in the maximum-security camps. Having no tangible goals to motivate them in the minimum-security prisons, several of our young servicemen pulled the covers up over their heads and died for no apparent reason other than the absence of a cause to live for.

If you don't know where you're going, it doesn't make any difference if the alarm clock goes off in the morning. If you don't stand for something, you'll fall for anything. But if your goals are vivid, specific, flexible, and supported by action plans and subgoals, you'll believe that your life is worth living. And you'll be right.

Turn Obstacles into Opportunities

Gail Devers, the Olympic sprint champion from my home-town of San Diego, has had to overcome more chaos and more obstacles to her goals than any other athlete I'm aware of.

Gail's problems appeared suddenly in 1988, her final year at UCLA. She suddenly began suffering agonizing migraine headaches, partial blindness, memory loss, and convulsions. For nearly two years she lived in constant pain and the doctors couldn't tell her why.

Finally, in 1990, her illness was diagnosed as Graves' disease, which could have resulted in cancer if it had gone untreated for even another few weeks. During radiation and chemotherapy, Gail's feet began to swell and blister. The pain was so great she couldn't walk, and when she tried to crawl, skin rubbed off her knees. Doctors later told her if she had continued trying to walk, her feet might have had to be amputated in order to save her life. This chaotic situation took place a little more than a year before the 1992 Olympic Games in Barcelona.

In March 1991, Gail's condition finally began to improve.

Most of us would have been happy just to be alive, but Gail began a flextactics approach to Olympic sprint training. Because she couldn't run, Gail took a stationary bike onto the field and peddled relentlessly while her teammates raced around the track.

But within a month, she was able to walk, in sweat socks, around the track at UCLA. A few months later, Gail was running competitively, and a year later she was at the Olympics in Barcelona. She was not the favorite in the 100-meter dash, but she won the gold in the fastest time of her career.

Heading for a certain second gold-medal performance in the 100-meter hurdles, Gail's speed was so great that she hit the last hurdle, fell to the ground, and crawled across the finish line, out of contention. Many athletes would have been emotionally crushed by an accident like that, but Gail Devers saw it as just one of those chaotic things that demand a flexible response. As she put it, "Going through what I've gone through, there's no obstacle I can't overcome."

Be Selective to Gain the Most from Today

When you really focus on what you want to accomplish, you can get more done in a single day than most people can in a month.

Although the clock is always running, we can use it as we choose. We can choose how long we work, how long we play, how long we watch TV, how long we rest, how long we worry, and how long we procrastinate. We can't always completely control our work schedules, but we can establish our priorities each day. Get up thirty to forty minutes earlier in the morning and decide what you're going to do during the day that will move you closer to your major goals. Make your phone calls at certain times, receive incoming calls at other times, handle each piece of correspondence just once, and delegate all work that can't stand up to the test of "Is this the best use of my time right now?"

If you watch extraordinarily productive people, you soon discover that their secret lies in the creation of an efficient daily routine, not in their talent or even in their genius. Successful people are *selective* people who have learned to get the most from each day.

Think Positively About Your Work

A very revealing five-year study of leading scholars, artists, and athletes was conducted by the University of Chicago under the supervision of Dr. Benjamin Bloom. The research was based on anonymous interviews with twenty outstanding performers in various fields, including concert pianists, Olympic swimmers, tennis players, sculptors, and mathematicians. Dr. Bloom and his team of researchers probed for clues as to how these achievers had developed.

The final report stated conclusively that drive and determination, not great natural talent, led to the outstanding success of these individuals. Dr. Bloom noted, "We expected to find tales of great natural gifts. We didn't find that at all. Their mothers often said it was another child who had the greater talents." There were, however, extraordinary accounts of hard work and dedication, such as the pianist who practiced several hours a day for seventeen years, and the swimmer who rolled out of bed every morning at half past five to do laps for two hours before school.

In all areas of life, joy in success comes in proportion to the amount of effort expended to achieve it. In order to make a maximum effort consistently, you should be passionate about your chosen profession—and if you're not, you should probably change professions. If you can't actually love your work, try to find something new and stimulating in it every day, and keep developing new and better ways to gain optimum results. Instead of "Thank God it's Friday," think how fortunate you are to be making a contribution where you're needed and employed every day of the week.

Find Goals That Benefit Yourself and Others

On the day she was born, her father was in a federal courthouse in Tucson, Arizona, battling lawyers from three states in a court case that had been going on for ten years. Her father commented, "After dealing with slick lawyers for that long, I'd like to have a little legal advice somewhere in the family."

Young Sandra Day must have taken those remarks to heart. While she was growing up in Arizona, she spent one summer vacation visiting a number of state capitols. She remembers standing on the steps and imagining what it would be like to come to work every day in such impressive buildings. She was sixteen when she graduated from high school and applied to only one college—Stanford. But though she eventually graduated with honors from Stanford Law School, she had difficulty finding a job because of the legal profession's prejudice against women at the time.

Since she was being offered only entry-level positions as a legal secretary, Sandra turned to a career in public service, which had always been her goal. She said she would rather help people and see justice prevail than become a partner in a private law firm anyway. After Sandra's brilliant career in public service and as a member of the Arizona State Senate, William French Smith, as attorney general, recommended her for the nation's highest judicial office. And in 1981, public servant Sandra Day O'Connor became the first woman justice of the United States Supreme Court.

Be Flexible in Your Expectations

In the summer of 1981, three friends named Ron Carrion, Jim Harris, and Bill Murto began flirting with the idea of starting a business. They weren't committed to any particular product or industry, and in fact their discussions were extremely wide-ranging. At various times they considered opening a Mexican restaurant, manufacturing a beeper device to help find lost car keys, and starting a computer firm. Gradually the computer idea began to seem more and more exciting, and this was the direction in which they finally decided to go. The original concept for the Compaq computer company was written on a place mat at a House of Pies restaurant in Houston, Texas.[9]

This may seem like flexibility of expectation carried to the extreme, and in a sense it was. Initially, the three friends were open to anything. On the other hand, their expectations were also very clearly focused. They knew they wanted to start a business that would be exciting, challenging, and profitable, but they just didn't know what it was yet. By opening their minds to any and all possibilities, they were able to discover their true needs. They saw something they wanted in the computer industry, and it was something that the key-beeper idea just didn't have.

Don't restrict yourself in the early stages of goal setting. Balance the need for clarity of purpose against the importance of being open-minded and flexible in your thinking. Don't become wedded to any idea until you've at least dated a few others.

Set New Standards When You Exceed Your Goals

By staying focused and flexible, you will meet and exceed your major life-forming goals. Thus, this tenth and final tactic encompasses all the rest. Success is not a resting place. It is a launching pad. Goal achievement is like a high school or college commencement ceremony. It is not the end of education, but the commencing or beginning of a lifelong journey into enlightenment and fulfillment.

When you think about your goals, don't focus on the road least traveled, or the road most traveled, but on the road *best* traveled. Think of a never-ending highway, one with magnificent vistas but with some detours and some ruts in the road as well.

Always remember that it's a highway with plenty of surprises along the way. Concentrate your energy on the quality of the journey. Enjoy the constant changes in the landscape. Expect the unexpected.

Above all, be inspired as you go by this timeless truth, that ''the road to heaven is heaven itself!''

The Twenty-one-Day Action Plan

The Action Plan that comprises the final section of this book can help you put twenty-first-century goal setting to work in your life immediately. The Plan includes practical applications for the flextactics we've discussed in previous chapters, as well as suggestions for using your journal as a tool for achieving both life-forming goals and preliminary subgoals. By following the Twenty-one-Day Action Plan, you can experience goal setting and goal achievement as an organized, well-thought-out undertaking. You'll have the sense of conscious control over your own life that is one of the key characteristics of peak performers in all fields. Rather than simply letting things happen to you, you'll be making things happen *for* you, starting today.

Remember, though, that flexibility is now one of the most important requirements for success. The Action Plan is not carved in stone. Don't feel that you have to follow the Plan to the letter if some of it feels unsuited to your current needs. Indeed, don't feel compelled to follow it at all if a different approach seems more appropriate—perhaps another type of Plan that you create yourself. In that case, the pages that follow can be looked upon simply as a list of suggestions. The purpose is to give you a hands-on feel for how goal setting actually works. Whether you follow this plan or not, however, I do think it's important for you to find an organized yet adaptable way of implementing the ideas in *The New Dynamics of Goal Setting* as soon as possible, while the experience of reading the book is still fresh in your mind. The techniques of the Twenty-one-Day Action Plan work for me, and I believe there's a good chance they'll work for you as well.

For all its challenges and occasional frustrations, we're fortunate to live in a time of virtually unlimited opportunity. In the last ten years, the entire world has suddenly opened up to new and previously undreamed-of ideas and possibilities. Regardless of what you want to accomplish, there has literally never been a better time to go after it.

All you need now is the notebook that will serve as your journal, and a pen or pencil. Believe me, you've already got everything else you need to achieve all your goals.

Day One

In carrying out this Action Plan, your first activity is in many ways your most important.

You are going to define your Life-Forming Goals and write them in your journal. And from now on, whenever you open your journal, you will always read over your Life-Forming Goals.

It is not, of course, "against the rules" to change these goals, but neither should such changes be made lightly. If you think carefully now about what you really want to accomplish, both personally and professionally, you will probably never need to change the Life-Forming Goals you are about to write.

Remember, the key to discovering your Life-Forming Goals lies in answering the following question: "If it weren't for money, time, and personal responsibilities, what would I really love to do with my life?"

Sometimes a Life-Forming Goal is very obvious. It may be something you think about every day, something that is always in the forefront of your consciousness. If such a Life-Forming Goal instantly springs to mind, by all means write it down.

But you may also find that you need to think more deeply to discover other of your fundamental objectives. If so, you may want to "revisit your childhood" for guidance, as we discussed in Chapter Three. To facilitate this, use the following questions as guidelines:

- What did you love to do as a child? What were you really good at? What made you feel proud?

- What makes you feel that way now?
- What have you done to benefit other people, that gave you a feeling of self-respect and fulfillment?

Take as much time as you need before writing anything down. I suggest dividing your Life-Forming Goals into two categories—Personal and Professional—and that you have no more than four goals in each. You may find it useful, however, to make a longer list, and then arrive at your final goals by process of elimination.

When, after searching your heart, you have finally defined your Life-Forming Goals and written them in your journal, you will have done a full day's work!

Day Two

Achieving your Life-Forming Goals is really a process of accomplishing a series of preliminary objectives. There are three types of these:

1. *Long-term Goals* are just one category short of the Life-Forming Goals that you wrote down on Day One. Long-term Goals, which usually take at least three years to accomplish, include major career, family, and financial plans. Providing for your retirement or your children's college education are examples of Long-term Goals.
2. *Intermediate Goals* normally require six months to three years for accomplishment. Purchasing a new home or getting a postgraduate degree are typical Intermediate Goals.
3. *Immediate Goals* are most often those that can be achieved within the next three to six months. For the purposes of this Plan, however, you will define two Immediate Goals—one Personal and one Professional—which you will achieve within twenty-one days.

Think carefully about the Immediate Goals you intend to achieve, and by the end of the day write them on a blank page of your journal. Then break the Immediate Goals into even smaller Personal and Professional subgoals that you can begin acting upon immediately. There can be lots of these subgoals—dozens, in fact! Write them in your journal as well. If you need more information about immediate goals and subgoals, read over Chapter Six.

Day Three

After reading over your Life-Forming Goals—as you do every day—look at the Personal and Professional Immediate Goals you wrote yesterday. Then ask yourself these flextactic questions:

- What risks will you need to take in order to achieve these goals by the time you reach the end of this Action Plan?
- What can you learn from your past that will help you accomplish these objectives?
- When you visualize yourself after you've attained these Immediate Goals, what do you see? Are you able to clearly and convincingly picture the benefits that you'll gain?

Also yesterday, you wrote down a number of Personal and Professional subgoals that you can act upon immediately. These should require some effort, but they need not interfere with your other responsibilities and priorities. They should be challenging, but not out of reach. The magnitude of the subgoal is much less important than the sense of accomplishment that comes from actually doing something that moves your life in the direction you want it to go.

Day Four

Goal setting is a learning experience as well as a practical technique for improving your life. If you accomplished the two subgoals you chose yesterday, congratulations! If you didn't, what can that teach you about yourself? What additional information will you need to achieve these subgoals? What habits and behaviors will you need to change?

Remember that one of our most important flextactics is the ability *to turn obstacles into opportunities*. This can refer to internal obstacles such as procrastination and fear as well as to objective barriers such as lack of time or funds. From now on, whenever you have a thought or feeling that seems negative or self-defeating, ask yourself, "Is this bringing me closer to my goals, or am I actually pushing them farther away?"

Now, as you move toward accomplishing your chosen Immediate Goals by the end of this Twenty-one-Day Action Plan, select two new subgoals that you intend to accomplish today. Or, if you didn't attain yesterday's subgoals, give them another try, armed with what you learned from your previous attempt. Most important, don't "beat yourself up" about any setbacks you may have experienced. A winner takes responsibility for his or her own destiny, but without lapsing into negative thought patterns. A winner knows that success is going to happen today . . . or if not today, tomorrow . . . or the day after that at the very latest!

Day Five

Choose a new pair of Personal and Professional subgoals that you intend to accomplish today.

- Remember the flextactic that says, *"Use your past to chart your future."* There's a very powerful variation of this for helping to put problems into perspective. Think back to two years ago. What problems were you facing at that time? Did they destroy you? Do they seem so all-important now? Do they seem important at all? Can you even recall them? You can be sure that in a very short time, today's difficulties will seem equally manageable, if not totally inconsequential. The present can function like a magnifying glass, distorting minor setbacks into major catastrophes. Don't let yourself be fooled!
- Think of the obstacles that stand between you and the Immediate Goals you intend to achieve by the end of this Plan. Do any of them exist more in your imagination than in the real world? What steps can you take to test the reality of these obstacles? If, for instance, you've been "sure" that a certain prospect will hang up on you if you call, test that assumption. You may be surprised by the result. And if he or she does in fact hang up on you, congratulate yourself on your knowledge of human nature!

Day Six

Today we'll focus on reflection and planning, rather than on selecting and achieving new subgoals. Begin by reading over the Personal Inventory entries in your journal, as described in Chapter Three. Pay special attention to the people you've designated as mentors, "sounding boards," and "springboards." Is there anyone you may have left out? If so, use this time for entering their names.

- Since you first made these entries in your journal, have you contacted anyone on your lists with the specific intention of sharing your goals and soliciting their advice and assistance?

- As a highly motivated, success-oriented person, it's important to surround yourself with like-minded people. This doesn't mean that all your friends have to agree with you about everything, but you should recognize the destructive influences of cynical, habitually negative individuals, and try to minimize their presence in your life. Or, better yet, see if there's anything you can do to help them achieve a more positive outlook.

- Set aside twenty to thirty minutes today to use the "power of visualization" flextactic, as discussed in Chapter Five. Imagine what a typical day will be like when you've achieved your Life-Forming Goals. Close your eyes and see this in as much detail as possible. At the same time, allow yourself to feel the inner satisfaction that will accompany your success.

Day Seven

As you look back over the week that's ending, are you satisfied that the majority of your actions were oriented toward bringing you closer to your chosen goals? Were you conscious of the long-term effects of the choices you made during the week? Right now, read over Chapter Eight (Flextactic: Be Selective to Gain the Most from Today) and follow the instructions below.

- Try to recall the things you accomplished in the past week that did the most to bring you closer to your Life-Forming Goals, and especially to the Personal and Professional Immediate Goals that you've chosen to attain by the end of this Twenty-one-Day Action Plan. Don't include the sub-goals that were consciously intended to have this effect. Focus on the beneficial things that you did during the everyday course of your life and work. List as many of these positive actions as you can remember.
- Can you also remember doing things during the week that had a negative effect on your goal achievement? There may have been times when you procrastinated, or gave in to fear and negative thinking. Make a list of these occasions—and be ruthlessly honest!
- Now compare the two lists. The first one should be considerably longer than the second. If it isn't, don't be discouraged—next week we'll be creating a new pair of lists, and you'll have a chance to improve your ratio of positive choices to negative ones.

Day Eight

Pick two new subgoals that you intend to accomplish today. These should be steps toward the Immediate Goals you've chosen to accomplish by the end of this Plan.

- Goal setting and achievement should never be a source of stress or displeasure. Rather, they should be exciting and fun. Be sure you're getting sufficient exercise and rest to minimize stress in your life. If you're not, what can you do to improve this? Right now, try to think of some specific steps you can take to relax and recharge.
- When you feel stressed, use the power of visualization (see Chapter Five) to restore balance. Think of all the times you've faced similar or even greater challenges and have achieved a successful outcome. Close your eyes and reexperience the satisfaction you felt at overcoming obstacles and attaining your objectives. Professional athletes watch personal-highlight films in order to build confidence and to maintain a positive attitude despite extreme pressure. You can do the same thing simply by closing your eyes!
- Remember: A high expectation of success is the best predictor of a positive result.

Day Nine

If you didn't achieve the Personal and Professional subgoals you selected yesterday, carry them over to today. If you did achieve them, pat yourself on the back and pick two new ones!

- *"Creating a blueprint for success"* (Chapter Six) means taking practical steps to move your life toward goal achievement. Sometimes, however, it's easy to overlook the practical influence of such things as your personal appearance, the neatness of your desk and your office, and even the presence of clutter in your car. Are you satisfied with the way you look? Are you aware of the importance that other people inevitably attach to your appearance?
- Your physical environment is both a cause and an effect of how you feel about yourself. If there are clothes in your closet or your drawers that you haven't worn in the last year, put them in a bag and donate them to an appropriate charity. If there are books on your shelves that you haven't read and are never going to read, give them to your local library. You can do the same with old audiocassettes and CDs. You'll be creating more positive surroundings for yourself, and helping others at the same time.

Day Ten

We're approaching the halfway point of this Twenty-one-Day Action Plan. As you do every day, read your Life-Forming Goals in your journal. Then pay special attention to the Personal and Professional Immediate Goals that you've targeted for completion by the end of the twenty-one days.

Are you satisfied with your progress? Select two new subgoals for today that can keep you on the right track!

- Look ahead to the next ten days. How can you "clear the decks" to create maximum flexibility and efficiency? Are there tasks that you've been putting off, or chores that you've been avoiding? Overlooking these things creates "mental clutter" and a subtle but powerful lowering of self-esteem. If there are bills to be paid, calls to be returned, or letters to be written, take care of them today!
- *"Think positively about your work"* is an important flex-tactic to remember when you deal with things that you've been avoiding. Always make an effort to look for the silver lining in every task, even the ones that may initially seem unpleasant. Look for the hidden benefits that you'll gain from finally having these things out of the way. Or try to turn them into a challenging and entertaining game. Reread Chapter Nine for more ideas on this.

Day Eleven

By now you should be used to the rhythm of achieving one Personal and one Professional subgoal each day. Congratulations! This puts you in the top 1 percent of peak performers.

By continuing to make a small but positive difference every day, you can accomplish virtually any goal!

- Creating a time log is one of the best ways to improve your productivity. Today, try keeping an itemized list of your activities, together with the times you began and ended them. Don't leave anything out, since the time required by even minor activities quickly adds up. You will probably be very surprised by what you learn.
- Time wasting—like all forms of negative behavior—usually requires the collaboration of others. Are you in the habit of turning meetings and phone calls into open-ended chat sessions? Without being rude, try to minimize this behavior in yourself and those around you. In other words, stay focused! For more thoughts on this subject, turn to Chapter Eight.

Day Twelve

In order to achieve your life's objectives, it's extremely important to understand the differences between ... Performance Goals and Outcome Goals. With Performance Goals, you compete against yourself. ... Outcome Goals are attained by competing against others. ...

—from Chapter Ten

Today we'll focus on Performance Goals rather than activities whose success or failure is determined by their outcome. Please follow the directions below:

- Think of some activities that you enjoy doing purely for their own sake. Though they may be work-related, they should be things that seem almost like play to you. Make a list in your journal of at least three such activities.
- As you look at your list, try to think of ways to combine these pastimes with your goal-directed activities. This may not be as difficult as you might at first imagine. If you enjoy playing or watching sports, for example, there may be someone on your list of ''sounding boards'' and ''springboards'' who shares your interest and would like to join you. Perhaps you could join a group devoted to your chosen activity, or take a class. Doing things that you really enjoy is never a waste of time, and meeting people in the course of such activities can be very positive both personally and professionally.
- ''Success is a process, not a destination.'' With this in mind, try to turn some of your Outcome Goals into Per-

formance Goals. If you're composing a business letter, for example, try to make it the best letter you can—in your own opinion, and just for the fun of it! The result will probably be far superior to what you would have attained by focusing on the possible responses of the recipient.

Day Thirteen

In keeping with our awareness of the importance of flexibility and risk taking, let's try some things that may take you out of your comfort zone, but that will probably broaden your horizon and stretch your mind.

- Look up ten new words in the dictionary and learn their meanings. During the day, try to use them in conversation, even if you feel a bit self-conscious. But watch out—this may become a habit!
- Buy an out-of-town newspaper and read the local news. Try to identify the differences and similarities between your area and the one you're reading about.
- Unplug your television set!
- If you're a male, identify something that's stereotyped as "woman's work" and go for it! Try baking a cake, for instance, or attempt to sew something. If you're female, identify a similarly male-specific activity and give it a whirl.

Day Fourteen

Earlier you were asked to make lists of the positive and negative activities you engaged in during the week. Today, as you make your new lists, has your positive-to-negative ratio improved?

There's one week left to attain the Personal and Professional Immediate Goals you selected at the start of the Twenty-one-Day Action Plan. As we begin the final week, make a resolution to eliminate self-sabotaging behavior and to replace it with thoughts and actions that bring you closer to your objectives. Put this in writing in your journal!

- If you sincerely feel that the Immediate Goals you selected are not realistic, feel free to adjust them without inflicting guilt upon yourself. Remember the flextactic discussed in Chapter Eleven: *"Be flexible in your expectations."* The key is to recognize the real reason for wanting to alter your goals. Is it because of new information you've gained, or is it the negative influence of habit and inertia?
- By the end of the day, you should have settled on Immediate Goals that you intend to achieve within the next week. Whether they're the same ones you originally selected is unimportant. What is important is your commitment to attaining them in the next seven days!

Day Fifteen

Begin this week by reading your Life-Forming Goals in your journal. Then read over the Personal and Professional Immediate Goals you intend to accomplish by next week. Then select two subgoals that are especially interesting, challenging, and effective—and make them happen today!

- Chapter Ten focused on finding *"goals that benefit yourself and others."* How will the achievement of your goals help other people? By thinking of your objectives in terms of their benefits to the world at large, you'll increase your motivation and your likelihood of success.
- Many successful companies create "vision statements" that express their goals succinctly and powerfully. These statements look beyond the obvious purpose of simply making money for the stockholders and the employees, to the larger purpose of the enterprise. In your journal, try writing a "vision statement" that articulates the true purpose of all your goal-directed behavior. Is it to provide a better life for your children, or to set a positive example for them? Is it simply to enhance your level of material comfort? Be honest with yourself. Ideally, the statement should be no more than twenty-eight words in length.
- Once you've formulated your vision statement, commit it to memory and repeat it to yourself several times each day to help keep focus and motivation high.

Day Sixteen

Have you had success in meeting (or networking by e-mail or fax) with your mentors, your "sounding boards," and your "springboards" in connection with achieving your goals? If you've been disappointed in your interactions with any of these individuals, don't take it personally. Sometimes even very well-intentioned people aren't in a position to extend themselves at a given moment. But you shouldn't hesitate to select new mentors who may be in a better position to help.

- What are the specific qualities that make you look up to a person? Are these the qualities that you *should* be looking up to as you strive to achieve your goals? Write down the five or six personal characteristics that ought to be present in someone whom you look to for help.
- What traits do you think other people see in you? Are you the kind of person who could be a mentor to someone following in your footsteps? List the half-dozen traits that come to mind as you try to describe yourself.
- If you're not happy with the list of your personal characteristics, start doing something about it today!

Day Seventeen

At the beginning of The New Dynamics of Goal Setting, *we met Jeff Sampson, the aeronautics engineer who was suddenly laid off from his job. Because of his flexible response, the layoff turned out to be the key to Jeff's success. Are you prepared for sudden changes that may contain hidden opportunities?*

- If the subgoals you've selected for today prove to be out of your reach, you simply move them ahead to tomorrow. This is a flexible response to a small setback. If a larger setback were to occur—if you were to lose your job, for instance—would you be able to find other employment? Or would you strike out on your own? Think about how you would respond to specific obstacles. Write your responses in your journal.

- When reverses occur in business or personal life, the effects are often magnified because people have never prepared themselves for how they might *feel* under such circumstances. This is something quite different from being technically or professionally prepared. Could you cope with sudden reversals without losing your all-important sense of self-respect?

- No matter what happens today, your responses are completely within your control. Just as the sun will rise tomorrow, you can maintain a positive attitude and a focus on your goals. Throughout history, every achiever has faced difficulties, and often sudden, unexpected ones. When such things happen to you, you're in good company!

Day Eighteen

There are only two more days in which to accomplish the Professional Immediate Goal you chose at the beginning of this Twenty-one-Day Action Plan. If you're close to attaining this objective, you should be very proud. In a matter of a few weeks, you've achieved something that normally takes at least several months. If it doesn't look like you're going to make it, perhaps you were too ambitious in your selection of an Immediate Goal. You can turn this setback into an opportunity by learning from this experience. Ambition is a good thing—but too much of a good thing can clog up the works!

- Are you a person who sees the glass as half full or as half empty? Do you focus on the probability of success or on the possibility of failure? As we approach the end of the Twenty-one-Day Action Plan, you should be able to learn a great deal about yourself in this regard.
- When you select two more subgoals to accomplish today, call upon the reserves of energy that all peak performers have, and commit yourself to making them happen.
- Winners enjoy celebrating their successes. When you succeed in accomplishing today's subgoals, present yourself with a reward. You may want to buy something you've wanted but have been putting off, or you may just want to relax by going to a pleasant restaurant or a good film. To make the experience even better, invite someone you care about to come with you. And be sure to mention the reason for the celebration: You attained your subgoals for the day!

Day Nineteen

If you've accomplished your chosen Immediate Goals ahead of schedule, you've shown that you have all the qualities necessary to achieve any objective. You're a budding superstar! Even if you have some work left to do, there are still three full days left in the Twenty-one-Day Action Plan.

Remember:

- You're never beaten until you stop trying.
- You are a peak performer as long as you do your best.
- The road to heaven is heaven itself.

Day Twenty

Use today as a "catch-up day" to accomplish whatever remains undone toward achieving your Personal and Professional Immediate Goals. As you do so, bear in mind that this Twenty-one-Day Action Plan is principally a learning experience, to familiarize you with the mechanics of goal setting and the degree of focus and discipline it requires. Regardless of whether you've achieved your objectives, the Plan is a success if you've gotten a sense of what it takes to be a winner, and what it feels like to win!

Today and every day:

- Read your Life-Forming Goals.
- Read your Long-term, Intermediate, and Immediate Goals and assess your progress toward them.
- Identify subgoals that you can achieve within the next twenty-four hours. These should be challenging but not impossible—just out of reach, but not out of sight.
- Be proud of your efforts toward maximum achievement. Be thankful for your successes, and thankful also for your defeats. The former are more fun, but the latter are often more informative.

Day Twenty-one

I hope that by today you've achieved your chosen Immediate Goals, but I hope even more that you've really tried. To teach you to do so, after all, is the fundamental purpose of this book. That was the goal I set for myself in writing the book, and with your help I hope I've succeeded. Thank you, and may all your achievements be as rewarding as this one was for me.

• Here is a list of the flextactics introduced in the preceding pages. Be sure to copy them in your journal:

—Make flexibility the key to your success.

—Learn to thrive on risk.

—Use your past to chart your future.

—Make your life an open book.

—Use the power of visualization.

—Create a blueprint for success.

—Turn obstacles into opportunities.

—Be selective to gain the most from today.

—Think positively about your work.

—Find goals that benefit yourself and others.

—Be flexible in your expectations.

—Set new standards when you exceed your goals.

SOURCES

1. Michael Treacy and Fred Wiersema, *The Discipline of Market Leaders* (Reading, MA: Addison-Wesley, 1995).
2. James Gleick, *Chaos: Making a New Science* (New York: Viking, 1987).
3. Jeremy Rifkin, *The End of Work* (New York: Tarcher/Putnam, 1995).
4. Dr. David Viscott, *Risking* (New York: Simon & Schuster, 1979).
5. *Business Week,* November 11, 1995.
6. Colin Powell, *My American Journey* (New York: Random House, 1995).
7. Sam Deep and Lyle Sussman, *Smart Moves* (Reading, MA: Addison-Wesley, 1990).
8. Jim Bolus, *Run for the Roses: 100 Years at the Kentucky Derby* (New York: Hawthorn Books, 1974).
9. Robert X. Cringely, *Accidental Empires* (Reading, MA: Addison-Wesley, 1992).